dk online

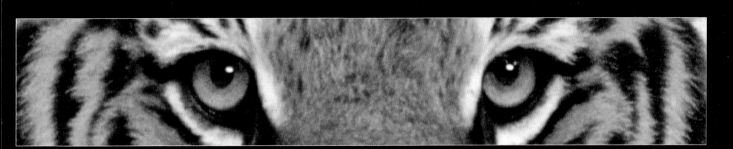

mammal

LONDON, NEW YORK, MELBOURNE,
MUNICH, and DELHI

Project Editor Belinda Weber
Senior Editor Clare Lister
Weblink Editors Niki Foreman, John Bennett

Managing Editor Linda Esposito

Digital Development Manager Fergus Day
DTP Co-ordinator Tony Cutting

Consultant Kim Bryan
Jacket Editor Mariza O'Keeffe

Publishing Managers Caroline Buckingham, Andrew Macintyre

Project Art Editor Rebecca Johns
Senior Designer Jim Green
Illustrators Mark Longworth, Andrew Kerr, Robin Hunter
Cartography Simon Mumford

Managing Art Editor Diane Thistlethwaite

Picture Research Carolyn Clerkin
Picture Librarians Sarah Mills, Rose Horridge, Karl Stange, Kate Ledwith

Production Erica Rosen
Jacket Designer Neal Cobourne

Art Director Simon Webb

First American hardback edition published in 2005
This paperback edition first published in 2007

Published in the United States by DK Publishing, Inc.,
375 Hudson Street, New York, New York 10014

05 06 07 08 09 10 9 8 7 6 5 4 3 2 1

Published in Great Britain by Dorling Kindersley Limited.

A catalog record for this book is available from the Library of Congress.

ISBN 978-0-75663-137-6

Color reproduction by Media Development and Printing, UK
Printed in China by Toppan Printing Co. (Shenzen) Ltd.

Discover more at
www.dk.com

dk online

mammal

Written by **Jen Green**
and **David Burnie**

Google

CONTENTS

How to use the Web site

DK online Mammal has its own Web site, created by DK and Google™. When you look up a subject in the book, the article gives you key facts and displays a keyword that links you to extra information online. Just follow these easy steps.

http://www.mammal.dkonline.com

1 Enter this Web site address…

Address : http://www.mammal.dkonline.com

2 Find the keyword in the book…

monotremes

3 Enter the keyword…

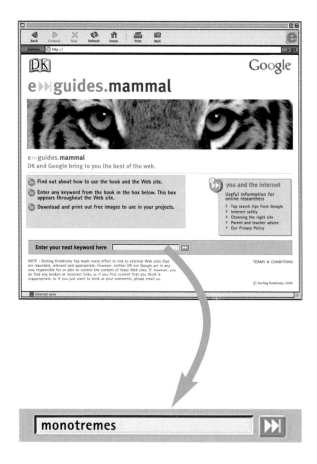

monotremes

You can use only the keywords from the book to search on our Web site for the specially selected DK/Google links.

Be safe while you are online:

- Always get permission from an adult before connecting to the internet.

- Never give out personal information about yourself.

- Never arrange to meet someone you have talked to online.

- If a site asks you to log in with your name or email address, ask permission from an adult first.

- Do not reply to emails from strangers—tell an adult.

Parents: Dorling Kindersley actively and regularly reviews and updates the links. However, content may change. Dorling Kindersley is not responsible for any site but its own. We recommend that children are supervised while online, that they do not use Chat Rooms, and that filtering software is used to block unsuitable material.

 **Click on your chosen link...**

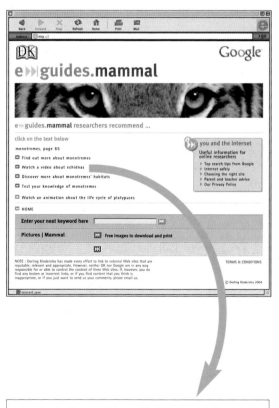

 **Download fantastic pictures...**

Pictures | Mammal

Lions

The pictures are free of charge, but can be used for personal non-commercial use only.

▶▶ **Watch a video about echidnas**

Links include animations, videos, sound buttons, virtual tours, interactive quizzes, databases, timelines, and realtime reports.

Go back to the book for your next subject...

WORLD OF MAMMALS

Mammals are perhaps the most familiar of all the animal groups, and the one to which we humans belong. From apes to aardvarks, and deer to dolphins, mammals are amazingly varied in size, form, and also lifestyle. Since humans first appeared, we have made use of other mammals for food, transportation, and to provide the materials for tools and clothing. Mammals are also important in nature. Meat-eating mammals reduce numbers of plant-eating animals that would otherwise strip habitats bare by eating all the new plant growth. Plant-eating mammals help to spread plants' seeds, and mammal dung fertilizes the soil.

Ears have a large surface area from which heat is lost to help keep the elephant cool

mammals

LARGEST ON LAND ▶
The mammal group includes the largest animal found on land, the African savannah elephant. A big male elephant can weigh almost 10 tons and have a shoulder height of up to 13 ft (4 m). The rhino is the world's second-largest land mammal, after the other elephants. At the other end of the scale, Kitti's hog-nosed bat is the smallest mammal, with a wingspan of 6 in (15 cm) and weighing just ½ oz (2 g). Several types of shrew are almost as tiny, with a body length of 1¾ in (4.5 cm), excluding the tail.

FINDING NEW SPECIES

Mammals are found almost everywhere on Earth, from dry land to the air and oceans. Some mammals inhabit harsh places such as snowy mountains and deserts; others live in rivers, dark caves, or underground. The mammal group contains more than 5,000 species. This total is still rising as new species are discovered—often in very remote places. Most discoveries are of small creatures, but in 1993, the saola was discovered in the dense forests of Vietnam. This hoofed mammal measures 5 ft (1.5 m) long and weighs 200 lb (90 kg). Some mammals live in large groups, while others are solitary except when they are raising young. Saola are thought to live alone or in small groups. They are an endangered species, threatened by hunting and loss of forest habitat.

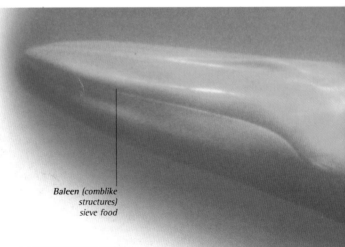

Baleen (comblike structures) sieve food

▲ LARGEST LIVING ANIMAL
Blue whales are the largest animals in the oceans, and indeed Earth's largest living animal. Females are larger than the males, and measure up to 110 ft (33 m) long and weigh up to 170 tons (150 metric tons). Even a newborn blue whale calf is 7 m (23 ft) long and weighs 2½ tons. However, blue whales are not the deepest-diving mammals. That record is held by the sperm whale, which descends to depths of up to 8,200 ft (2,500 m) when hunting. The Sei whale is the fastest whale, reaching speeds of up to 22 mph (35 kph) for short bursts.

SUCCESSFUL MAMMALS

DOMESTIC MAMMALS
Humans began to rear mammals for their meat, skin or wool more than 10,000 years ago. Goats, sheep, cattle, and pigs were among the first animals to be domesticated (tamed to live with humans). Dogs were probably the first pets. Later, oxen were used to pull ploughs, while horses and camels carried people or possessions.

NUMEROUS MAMMALS
Throughout history people have hunted mammals. This has made many species rare, and wiped out others altogether. Mammals such as rats and mice thrive alongside people. They are now among the world's most numerous mammals. Their ability to live in new surroundings and their fast breeding rate means that their numbers continue to grow.

ADAPTABLE MAMMALS
Most mammals have bodies adapted (suited) to living in a particular place. While the bodies of mammals such as whales are suited to dwelling in water, bats' front limbs have evolved into wings, which allow them to take to the air. By flying, bats can reach places other mammals cannot, and so they have less competition for food.

Pillar-like legs support heavy body

Savannah (tropical grasslands) are used for grazing by large herds of elephants and other mammals

Gigantic front flippers are used for steering

MAMMAL RECORD HOLDERS		
Largest mammal	Blue whale	Length: 33 m (110 ft) Weight: 150 tonnes (170 tons)
Largest land mammal	African elephant	Height 3.7 m (12 ft 2 in) Weight: 10 tonnes
Tallest land mammal	Giraffe	5.8 m (19 ft)
Fastest land mammal	Cheetah	100 kph (60 mph)
Slowest land mammal	Three-toed sloth	1.8–2.4 m (6 ft–7 ft 10 in) per minute
Fastest marine mammal	Commerson's dolphin	56 kph (35 mph)
Longest-lived mammal	Human, fin whale	100 years
Shortest-lived mammal	Shrew	9-12 months

WHAT ARE MAMMALS?

Mammals are a group of animals with an internal skeleton, including a backbone. Like birds, mammals are warm-blooded (able to generate and control their own body heat) and so can live in a wide variety of habitats. From bats to bears, and whales to wombats, all mammals share three key features that set them apart from other animals. First, all mammals have fur on their bodies. Second, all baby mammals are nourished by milk from their mothers. Third, all share a unique jaw structure, which scientists use to tell fossil mammals from other animals.

Long hairs on weasel's snout are touch sensitive

Fur has colors and patterns that provide camouflage

◄ MAMMAL HAIR
Mammals are unique among animals in possessing hair. In most species, like this weasel, a dense coat of hair covers almost all of the body. However, mammals that live in the oceans or hot places often have sparse hair, and certain whales posess it only before birth. Fur helps a mammal to keep warm and protects it against injury. In some mammals, long whiskers provide a sense of touch, while in porcupines and hedgehogs, hairs have become defensive spines.

Soles of feet are not covered with hair

Nose is not furry and loses body heat more quickly than furry areas

Thick fur reduces heat loss, saving energy

◄ WARM-BLOODED MAMMALS
All mammals can generate body heat, whatever the outside weather conditions. This is often called being warm-blooded, but endothermic is a more accurate term. Keeping an even temperature allows mammals like this polar bear to thrive in very cold places, such as the Arctic. Other mammals can remain active in hot places such as deserts. The disadvantage is that this process requires a great deal of energy, so mammals have to eat more food than cold-blooded animals like reptiles.

Fur has a layer of fat beneath that helps keeps body heat in

mammals

Umbilical cord

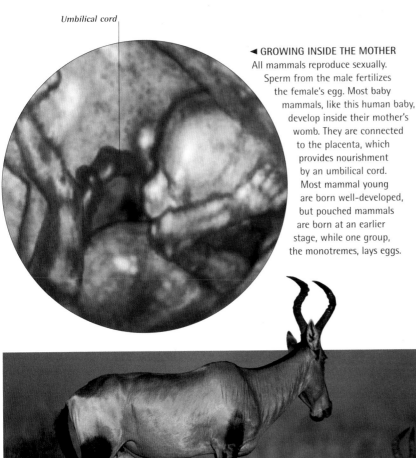

◀ GROWING INSIDE THE MOTHER
All mammals reproduce sexually.
Sperm from the male fertilizes
the female's egg. Most baby
mammals, like this human baby,
develop inside their mother's
womb. They are connected
to the placenta, which
provides nourishment
by an umbilical cord.
Most mammal young
are born well-developed,
but pouched mammals
are born at an earlier
stage, while one group,
the monotremes, lays eggs.

SHARED FEATURES

LION'S SKULL

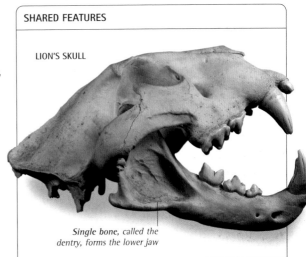

Single bone, called the
dentry, forms the lower jaw

A mammal's skeleton provides an inner framework for the body. All mammal skeletons share a similar basic structure, while being adapted to different habitats. The skull, like this lion skull, forms a protective case for the brain. Mammals are unique among animals in having a lower jawbone that hinges directly with the skull. This gives the jaw a powerful biting action. Both upper and lower jaws are armed with teeth that are suited to deal with the mammal's diet.

▲ NOURISHED BY MILK
All mammal mothers feed their babies on milk from the mammary glands. These skin glands, located on each side of the mother's chest or on her abdomen (belly), give the mammal group its name. Milk is a rich fluid that provides all the nourishment a baby like this red hartebeest needs. In addition, mammal mothers take more care of their young than other animals. The extended care offers many opportunities for the young to learn essential skills, such as finding food.

LIMB STRUCTURE

PORPOISE FORELIMB

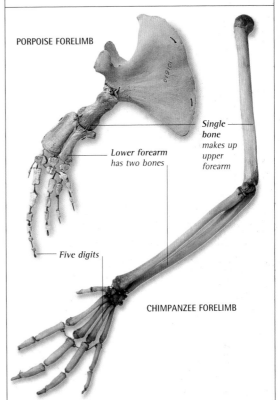

Lower forearm
has two bones

Single bone makes up upper forearm

Five digits

CHIMPANZEE FORELIMB

Almost all mammals have four limbs, but whales, including dolphins and porpoises, have lost their hind limbs, giving them a more streamlined shape. Different species have evolved to live in completely different environments, and their limbs have developed to aid movement in that particular habitat. The limbs of mammals as varied as chimpanzees and porpoises share a common pattern (as shown above), while individual bones have different shapes. The upper forelimb is made up of a single bone, while the lower part has two bones. Both end in five digits (fingers), which consist of many bones.

▲ INTELLIGENCE AND COMMUNICATION
Mammals have larger brains in relation to their body size than other animals. A well-developed brain processes information from the senses and gives a mammal the ability to change its behavior in response to changing conditions, which helps with survival. Primates like these chimpanzees are skilled communicators, living in complex social groups.

▲ DIMETRODON
Dating from the Early Permian period, Dimetrodon was up to 11 ft (3.5 m) long. This spectacular predator belonged to a group of reptiles called pelycosaurs, which were close relatives of the cynodonts. Dimetrodon had scaly skin like typical reptiles, but it also had two different types of teeth—something that made it more like a mammal.

ORIGIN OF MAMMALS

Mammals came about through evolution, a process of change that affects all living things. Their ancestors evolved from primitive fish. By the end of the Paleozoic Era, 250 million years ago, these animals gave rise to reptiles—a group that produced the dinosaurs. But before then, a group of reptiles called cynodonts developed some remarkable new features, including specialized teeth, jaws with fewer bones, and fur. About 200 million years ago, the first true mammals appeared.

▲ CYNOGNATHUS
This fossilized skull belonged to Cynognathus, one of the largest cynodonts, which was up to 3 ft 3 in (1 m) long. Cynognathus means "dog jaw"—a good description as it had teeth like a modern dog, including long canines that gripped its prey. For its size, its head was massive, and it would have had a wide gape and an extremely powerful bite.

evolution

Body covered in fur

Jaw made of a single bone

Digits end in sharp claws

▲ THRINAXODON
About the size of a cat, Thrinaxodon was a cynodont that lived during the Early Triassic period—the time when the first dinosaurs evolved. It had many mammal-like features, including specialized teeth, and a new kind of jaw that gave it a more powerful bite. It was probably covered with fur and likely to have been warm-blooded.

MAMMAL EVOLUTION TIMELINE

PHANEROZOIC EON—AGE OF ABUNDANT EVIDENT LIFE					
PALEOZOIC—AGE OF ANCIENT LIFE			MESOZOIC—AGE OF DOMINANT REPTILES		
PERMIAN PERIOD			TRIASSIC PERIOD		
EARLY	MIDDLE	LATE	EARLY	MIDDLE	LATE
292–275 million years ago (mya)	275–260 mya	260–251 mya	251–245 mya	245–228 mya	228–200 mya

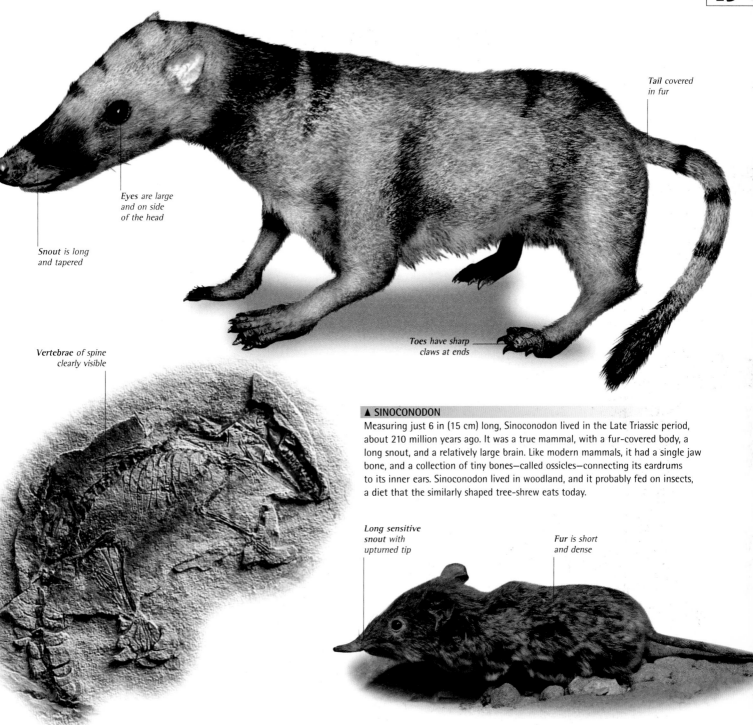

Tail covered in fur

Eyes are large and on side of the head

Snout is long and tapered

Vertebrae of spine clearly visible

Toes have sharp claws at ends

▲ SINOCONODON

Measuring just 6 in (15 cm) long, Sinoconodon lived in the Late Triassic period, about 210 million years ago. It was a true mammal, with a fur-covered body, a long snout, and a relatively large brain. Like modern mammals, it had a single jaw bone, and a collection of tiny bones—called ossicles—connecting its eardrums to its inner ears. Sinoconodon lived in woodland, and it probably fed on insects, a diet that the similarly shaped tree-shrew eats today.

Long sensitive snout with upturned tip

Fur is short and dense

▲ EOMAIA

Discovered in 2002 in northern China, this fossilized Eomaia is the earliest known ancestor of placental mammals. It dates from the Early Cretaceous period. Placentals produce live young, and they nourish their young inside their bodies for longer than other mammals. This new way of reproducing proved to be very successful. Today, placentals make up more than 90 percent of all mammals.

▲ ZALAMBDALESTES

By the Late Cretaceous period, true mammals were common, although very few of them reached a large size. Zalambdalestes was a typical example, measuring about 8 in (20 cm) long. With its pointed snout and long skull it looked similar to a modern-day shrew. It had long leg bones with nonopposable toes (unable to touch the ends of the other toes), which means it probably lived on the ground.

PHANEROZOIC EON—AGE OF ABUNDANT EVIDENT LIFE				
MESOZOIC—AGE OF DOMINANT REPTILES				
JURASSIC PERIOD			CRETACEOUS PERIOD	
EARLY	MIDDLE	LATE	EARLY	LATE
200–176 mya	176–161 mya	161–146 mya	146–99 mya	99–65 mya

EVOLUTION AND DIVERSIFICATION

At the end of the Cretaceous Period, 65 million years ago, a giant meteor hit the Earth, bringing the Age of Reptiles to an end. Most large land animals were wiped out. As life slowly recovered from this catastrophe, mammals replaced reptiles as the world's dominant animals. By the start of Pleistocene times, 1.8 million years ago, all of today's mammal groups had appeared. They included woolly mammoths and rhinos, and also toolmaking primates that walked upright—the ancestors of the human race.

DIPROTODON ▶

Almost as big as a modern-day hippo, Diprotodon was a giant marsupial (pouched mammal) that evolved in Oligocene times. It lived in Australia, an island continent that was gradually drifting away from other continents, isolating the pouched mammals from contact with other mammals. Diprotodon was a browser. It fed on saltbushes and other shrubs, tearing off leafy branches with its sharp front teeth.

Large jaws for chewing tough plants

Young carried in pouch made of elastic skin

Bearlike feet with large soles

▲ PROPALAEOTHERIUM

This superbly preserved fossil, from a quarry in Messel in Germany, shows the earliest true horse, which dates back to Eocene times. About the size of a large dog, it had a small head and hoofed feet with three or four toes. As horses evolved, they gradually became bigger and some of their toes disappeared.

Teeth used to stab prey

◀ EUSMILUS

During mammal evolution, predators with saber-shaped teeth evolved several times. They included saber-toothed marsupials and many kinds of saber-toothed cats. Eusmilus, from Oligocene times, was an early example. Altogether, it had just 26 teeth—18 fewer than typical cats today. Eusmilus's upper canines were enormous and projected far below its jaw when its mouth was closed.

MAMMAL EVOLUTION TIMELINE

PHANEROZOIC EON—AGE OF ABUNDANT EVIDENT LIFE			
CENOZOIC—AGE OF MAMMALS			
TERTIARY PERIOD			
PALEOCENE EPOCH	EOCENE EPOCH	OLIGOCENE EPOCH	MIOCENE EPOCH
65–54.8 mya	54.8–33.5 mya	33.5–24 mya	24–5.3 mya

Stones
shaped by
striking them
against each
other

◄ HOMO HABILIS

Homo habilis, or handy man,
lived in Africa and evolved about
2.5 million years ago. It belonged
to a family of primates called
hominids, which also includes
ourselves. It had a large brain and
was skilled at making stone tools—
a giant step in mammal evolution.
Homo habilis is one of at least
13 extinct hominids that
scientists have discovered.

▲ CETOTHERIUM

Mammals evolved on land, but by Miocene times many kinds had
taken up life in the sea. Early whales had long snouts and four
flipperlike legs, but later ones—such as Cetotherium—had front
flippers only and a horizontail tail. Cetotherium fed by filtering
small animals out of the water, just like most large whales do
today. Whales evolved from early hoofed mammals.

Fur is often found
preserved in fossils

evolution

WOOLY MAMMOTH ►

Pleistocene times ushered in a dramatic change
in climate, as the Earth cooled and a series of Ice
Ages began. In the northern hemisphere, where
the ice sheets were largest, mammals evolved
special adaptations (features) for coping with the
cold. The woolly mammoth had a thick coat of fur,
a short tail, and unusually small ears to prevent
loss of heat. Woolly mammoths roamed the
treeless tundra (barren lowlands) of Europe,
Asia, and North America.

Trunk used for
collecting food

PHANEROZOIC EON—AGE OF ABUNDANT EVIDENT LIFE		
CENOZOIC—AGE OF MAMMALS		
	QUATERNARY PERIOD	
PLIOCENE EPOCH	PLEISTOCENE EPOCH	HOLOCENE EPOCH
5.3–1.8 mya	1.8–0.01 mya	0.01 mya–present

MAMMAL GROUPS

There are more than 5,100 species of mammal on Earth today, and they live in all types of habitat. To make sense of this incredible diversity, scientists classify them in groups, in a way that shows how they are related by evolution. One group, called the monotremes, contains mammals that lay eggs. These are found only in Australasia. Next up in size, with about 300 species, are the metatheria or marsupials, which raise their young in a pouch. Finally there are the placental mammals, which nourish their young inside their bodies until they are fairly well-developed. There are more than 4,700 species of placentals, and they live all over the world.

MAMMAL CLASSIFICATION (*See also pp 90–91*)

PROTOTHERIA

EGG LAYING MAMMALS	FAMILIES	SPECIES
Monotremata	2	5

METATHERIA

POUCHED MAMMALS	FAMILIES	SPECIES
Didelphimorphia	1	78
Paucituberculata	1	6
Microbiotheria	1	1
Dasyuromorphia	2	71
Notoryctemorphia	1	2
Peramelemorphia	2	22
Diprotodontia	8	136

EUTHERIA

PLACENTAL MAMALS	FAMILIES	SPECIES
Carnivora	11	283
Pinnipedia (Carnivora)	3	34
Cetacea	11	83
Sirenia	2	4
Primates	10	372
Scandentia	1	19
Dermoptera	1	2
Proboscidea	1	3
Hyracoidea	1	6
Tubulidentata	1	1
Perissodactyla	3	20
Artiodactyla	10	228
Rodentia	24	2,105
Lagomorpha	2	83
Macroscelidea	1	15
Insectivora	6	451
Chiroptera	18	1,033
Xenarthra	5	31
Pholidota	1	7

DIPROTODONTIA ▶
Like all metatheria, koalas are born when they are still at an early stage of development. At birth, a young koala weighs about 100,000 times less than its mother. It clambers into its mother's pouch and spends up to six months inside it, feeding on her milk. After this, it rides on her back. Koalas have roomy pouches, but in some marsupials the pouch is very small and the young hang outside it, attached to their mother's teats. Metatheria are found in Australasia and the Americas.

◀ MONOTREMATA
The short-nosed echidna is the most common monotreme, or egg-laying mammal. Like its two relatives—the long-nosed echidna and the platypus—it lays small eggs with leathery shells. Once an echidna egg has hatched, the young animal spends its first eight weeks inside its mother's pouch, before starting to venture into the outside world. Platypuses do not have a pouch. Instead, the mother nurses her young inside the safety of a burrow.

CHIROPTERA ▶
Bats make up one of the largest groups of placental mammals, with nearly 1,000 species. They include the world's smallest mammals, weighing a fraction of a gram, and species like this flying fox, which has a wingspan of more than 5 ft (1.5 m). All bats are nocturnal, and most of them feed on insects, catching them by echolocation—a way of "seeing" that uses sound. Flying foxes feed mainly on fruit.

mammals

Nose gives flying foxes a good sense of smell

Wing membranes connect hind legs and tail

Wings are supported by long arm and finger bones

Large eyes give hyrax good eyesight

Ears fold flat when inside burrow

◀ HYRACOIDEA
The 11 species of hyraxs make up a small and distinctive family of placental mammals. With their stubby bodies, they look similar to guinea pigs, but their closest living relatives are elephants and sea mammals called dugongs and manatees. Hyraxes are good climbers thanks to their unusual toes, which are tipped with rubbery pads. They can survive with very little water, getting moisture from their food.

◀ TUBULIDENTATA
The aardvark is a placental mammal but it has no close relatives, so it is classified in an order all of its own. With its powerful claws, it is one of the fastest diggers in the mammal world. Aardvarks eat ants and termites, lapping them up with a long sticky tongue. Young aardvarks are born after a gestation period (the time between mating and birth) of eight months and are fairly well-developed at birth.

Scales grow continuously and are periodically replaced

◀ PHOLIDOTA
With their overlapping scales, pangolins look like walking pinecones. They live on insects and use their scales to protect themselves against attack. If they are threatened, pangolins coil up in a ball, with their heads tucked safely inside. Pangolins are placental mammals, and their young are born with soft scales—but these harden after a few weeks. There are seven species of pangolin, and they all live in Africa and southern Asia.

MAMMAL SKELETONS

Like birds, fish, frogs, and reptiles, mammals are vertebrates (backboned animals), with an internal skeleton to support their bodies. Mammals have the most complicated skeletons of any animal, which allow them to perform a wide range of movements. In addition to providing a framework for the body, the skeleton protects inner organs and anchors muscles, which pull on bones to create movement. The bones also store minerals and produce blood cells. All mammals have more than 200 bones in their bodies, though some of these are fused together. Bones are made of living tissue.

e ▶▶

skeletons

SKULL AND TEETH

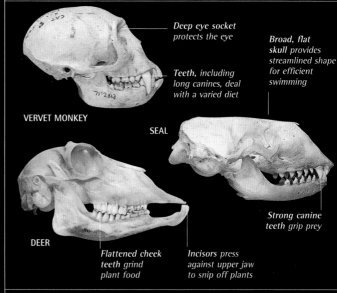

Deep eye socket protects the eye

Teeth, including long canines, deal with a varied diet

Broad, flat skull provides streamlined shape for efficient swimming

VERVET MONKEY

71ᵉ2313

SEAL

DEER

Flattened cheek teeth grind plant food

Incisors press against upper jaw to snip off plants

Strong canine teeth grip prey

The skull is a bony case that protects a mammal's brain. It also houses the main sense organs: the eyes, ears, tongue, and nasal passages. The jaws and also teeth of different mammals are adapted to suit their particular diet. Unlike other animals, mammals possess specialized teeth of four main types: front teeth called incisors for cutting, side teeth called canines for gripping, and cheek teeth called molars and premolars for grinding. However, not all mammals have all four kinds. The hinge joint of the jaw is one of the strongest in the body.

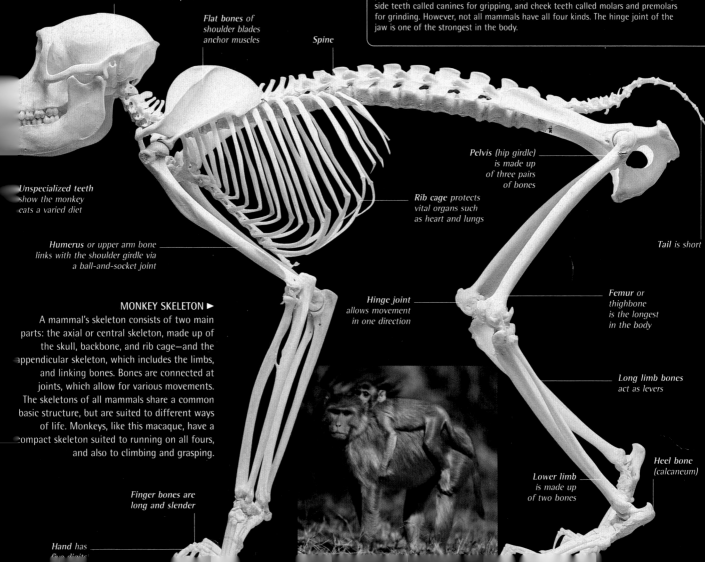

Skull is dome shaped

Flat bones of shoulder blades anchor muscles

Spine

Pelvis (hip girdle) is made up of three pairs of bones

Rib cage protects vital organs such as heart and lungs

Tail is short

Unspecialized teeth show the monkey eats a varied diet

Humerus or upper arm bone links with the shoulder girdle via a ball-and-socket joint

Hinge joint allows movement in one direction

Femur or thighbone is the longest in the body

Long limb bones act as levers

MONKEY SKELETON ▶

A mammal's skeleton consists of two main parts: the axial or central skeleton, made up of the skull, backbone, and rib cage—and the appendicular skeleton, which includes the limbs, and linking bones. Bones are connected at joints, which allow for various movements. The skeletons of all mammals share a common basic structure, but are suited to different ways of life. Monkeys, like this macaque, have a compact skeleton suited to running on all fours, and also to climbing and grasping.

Finger bones are long and slender

Heel bone (calcaneum)

Lower limb is made up of two bones

Hand has five digits

SKULL AND BACKBONE OF A FOX

Bones of skull form bony case called the cranium

Cervical (neck) vertebrae (almost all mammals have seven of these)

LIMB BONES ▶

Mammals' limb bones share a similar structure, but the exact shapes vary to suit different ways of life. The seal's limbs have evolved into powerful paddles that sweep the water aside. The gray seal's front flippers are mainly used for steering, while the powerful hind flippers provide locomotion. The forelimbs of other mammals are suited to different movements, including flying, running, hopping, and digging.

FRONT FLIPPER OF A SEAL

Large first finger at leading edge of flipper

Elongated digits

Radius

Ulna

Humerus or upper arm

Scapula or shoulder blade

◀ SPINAL COLUMN

The backbone is the central part of a mammal's skeleton, to which the skull and limbs are attached. It is made up of many small, wedge-shaped bones called vertebrae, which fit together to form a slender column. The backbone protects the spinal cord inside it. This is the main nerve bundle that connects the brain with other parts of the body. Bony projections (knobs) on the vertebrae make them interlock, and also anchor muscles.

Vertebrae of the back are divided into thoracic (upper) and lumbar (lower) region

Horses have between 14 and 21 tail vertebrae

BONES FROM HORSE'S TAIL

◀ TAILS

Most mammals have tails, which are supported by the caudal vertebrae. These bones vary in number, depending on the length. Tails are useful in many ways. The horse uses its tail as a flyswatter and to show its mood. The beaver's tail is used as a rudder and sometimes a paddle and signals alarm if slapped on the water. The lemur's tail can be waved like a flag to send messages to group members.

Lower tail vertebrae are slender

SPINE, LIMBS, AND MOVEMENT

RIGID SPINE
The horse's spine is relatively rigid. With its long legs, a horse is built for speed, and its spine aids endurance. The fairly inflexible spine saves on the energy used up with every stride, allowing the horse to run for a long time. Each foot has just a single toe, which has evolved into a hoof, with a hard outer part surrounding a cushioned sole. The horse is an unguligrade mammal—it runs on the tip of its toe.

FLEXIBLE SPINE
Predators like this tiger rely on bursts of speed to catch their prey. The spine is very flexible, coiling and uncoiling with each stride. This increases the animal's speed, but uses lots of energy, so the tiger cannot maintain its charge for long. The powerful limbs are also used for leaping, pouncing, climbing, and swimming. Tigers have five digits on their forefeet, four on their hind feet and are digitigrade—run on their toes.

Sacral (hip region) vertebrae are connected to the lower limbs via the pelvis

Caudal vertebrae form the tail

CANADIAN BEAVER TAIL

RING-TAILED LEMUR TAIL

Long, stiff whiskers are touch-sensitive

Pale guard hairs stick out beyond darker underfur

▲ TWO LAYERS OF FUR
All mammals have some hair on their bodies, and most have thick fur. Many, such as this Virginia opossum, are densely furred, leaving only the tip of the snout, soles of the feet, and tail bare. The fur of the opossum and many other species consists of two layers: an outer layer of long, coarse guard hairs and an underlayer of dense, fine fur. Guard hairs keep out cold, wind, and rain, while underfur traps air to insulate and warm the body.

Long tail lacks fur and is sensitive to touch

SKIN AND HAIR

Two of the main features that distinguish mammals from other animals are skin and hair. These are found at the surface of the body. Mammal skin contains many unique and vital glands, including mammary glands that provide milk to nourish young and sweat glands that help keep mammals cool. Hair, also unique to mammals, has many different uses. A hairy coat helps mammals to maintain a constant body temperature. It also protects against the elements and gives camouflage. In some mammals, hair has evolved into spiny prickles, or skin into a tough hide that forms a natural body armor.

Thick wool protects alpaca from cold

◄ ALPACA WOOL
Alpacas are domesticated members of the camel family from the Andes Mountains in South America. They possess a thick fleece of springy wool that traps abundant air to insulate the animal from wind and cold. Sheep and other camelids, such as llamas, that are found in mountain areas also have a woolly fleece. For thousands of years, these mammals have been bred for their wool, as well as for meat, milk, and hides.

TYPES OF HAIR AND FUR

SEAL FUR
Hair or fur has different lengths and textures in different mammal species. Seal fur is short and coarse. It protects the seal from scratching itself on the rocks when on land. Sebaceous glands in the skin produce oils that help to keep the coat waterproof when swimming.

COLOBUS MONKEY FUR
Colobus monkeys have soft, silky coats with long hairs. In the West African forests and woodlands, their dense fur protects them against rain and fierce tropical sunlight. It also helps camouflage these primates, enabling them to hide among the leaves of the shady canopy.

BEAVER FUR
Beavers spend much of their time in water. The long, pale guard hairs and dense underfur keep the animals dry while swimming and diving. These mammals were once plentiful by lakes and rivers in North America, but were overhunted for their fur and are now much rarer.

LYNX FUR
The spots on the lynx's coat help break up the big cat's outline, disguising it as it stalks its prey. The coat is long and thick with tufts on the ear tips. These tufts are particularly noticeable in the winter. The lynx also has long fur on its feet that helps movement in the snow.

HUMAN HAIR
Like all mammal hair, human hair consists of long rods of cells joined and strengthened by a substance called keratin. Humans have two main types of hairs: coarse head hair and fine hairs over the rest of the body that are automatically raised to trap insulating air when we get cold.

HAIRY HORN

Horn made of modified hair

Rhinoceroses have one or two horns on their head, depending on the species. The horn is actually modified hair, made of the tough protein keratin, which is also found in human hair and nails. Both male and female rhinos possess horns. The horns of cattle have a bony core and grow from the frontal bones of the skull. In contrast, rhino horns have no bony core. They grow from a roughened patch over the nasal bone. Rhino horns are used to intimidate predators and other rhinos.

Along with elephants and aquatic mammals such as whales, rhinos have few hairs on their bodies. The lack of hair suits life in a warm climate. The rhino's tough hide, up to 3/4 in (2 cm) thick, protects against thorns and also against attack from predators.

skin and hair

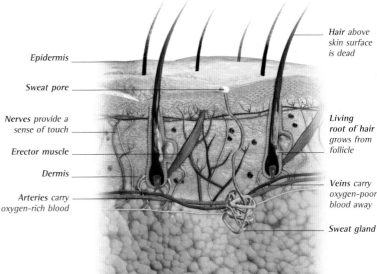

Hair above skin surface is dead

Epidermis

Sweat pore

Nerves provide a sense of touch

Erector muscle

Dermis

Arteries carry oxygen-rich blood

Living root of hair grows from follicle

Veins carry oxygen-poor blood away

Sweat gland

▲ INSIDE HUMAN SKIN
The skin of humans and other mammals consists of two layers. The epidermis or outer layer protects the dermis beneath. This dermis contains blood vessels, which supply the skin with blood, and nerves, which provide our sense of touch. Hairs growing from pits called follicles are raised by erector muscles to trap a layer of air. Sweat glands give off a salty liquid that helps draw heat from the skin.

Scratching helps to dislodge dirt and flakes of skin

◄ KEEPING CLEAN
Mammals, such as this rat, keep their fur clean and in good condition by licking it with the tongue, combing it with claws, and nibbling at it. This is called grooming. In many species, one animal grooms another. Social grooming strengthens bonds within the group.

◄ SHEDDING HAIR
Bactrian camels from the windswept wastes of Mongolia in central Asia have a long, shaggy coat suited to the harsh climate. In the fall, the animal grows an extrathick coat to keep it warm in the severe winter conditions. In the spring, this coat is shed or molted in patches and a lighter, thinner coat grows in its place. The camel looks scruffy and unkept until its molt is complete.

INSIDE MAMMALS

Mammals are incredibly diverse in size and shape, but all their bodies work in similar ways. All have a well-developed brain, complex senses, and a flexible skeleton to which muscles are attached. Other organs (working parts) include the heart, lungs, liver, and kidneys. Mammals' bodies are made up of tiny units called cells, which are grouped into tissues that combine to form organs. These organs work together to make body systems including the digestive system, respiratory system, circulatory system, and nervous system.

▲ RESPIRATION
All mammals need oxygen so that their cells can function and produce energy. The respiratory (breathing) system that allows mammals to absorb oxygen includes the lungs, nostrils, and trachea (windpipe). Mammals have a muscular diaphragm between their chest and abdomen, which contracts (tightens) to draw air into the lungs. This whale's blowhole (nostril) lies on top of its head.

Kidney removes waste products from the blood

ANATOMY ▶
All land mammals have four limbs, adapted to two- or four-legged movement and to flight in bats, but cetaceans (whales, dolphins, and porpoises) have lost their hind limbs. Many important organs are located in the thorax region near the forelimbs, while kidneys, intestines, and reproductive organs lie in the abdomen, near the hind limbs. Despite internal similarities, mammals differ greatly in their outer appearance. For example, elephants are distinguished by a long trunk, large ears, and tough skin.

Backbone is made up of many interlocking bones called vertebrae

Inner skeleton, or endoskeleton, gives the body shape and support

Intestines are part of the digestive process, absorbing nutrients (nourishment) from food

Limbs are sturdy to support the elephant's great weight

▲ DIGESTION
The digestive system breaks down food so nutrients can be absorbed into the body. It consists of a long tube down which food passes from the mouth to the stomach and intestines. Special muscles in the walls of the digestive tract (tube) tighten to push food along it. Waste from food leaves the body via the anus. Rabbits have special microbes to help them break down cellulose.

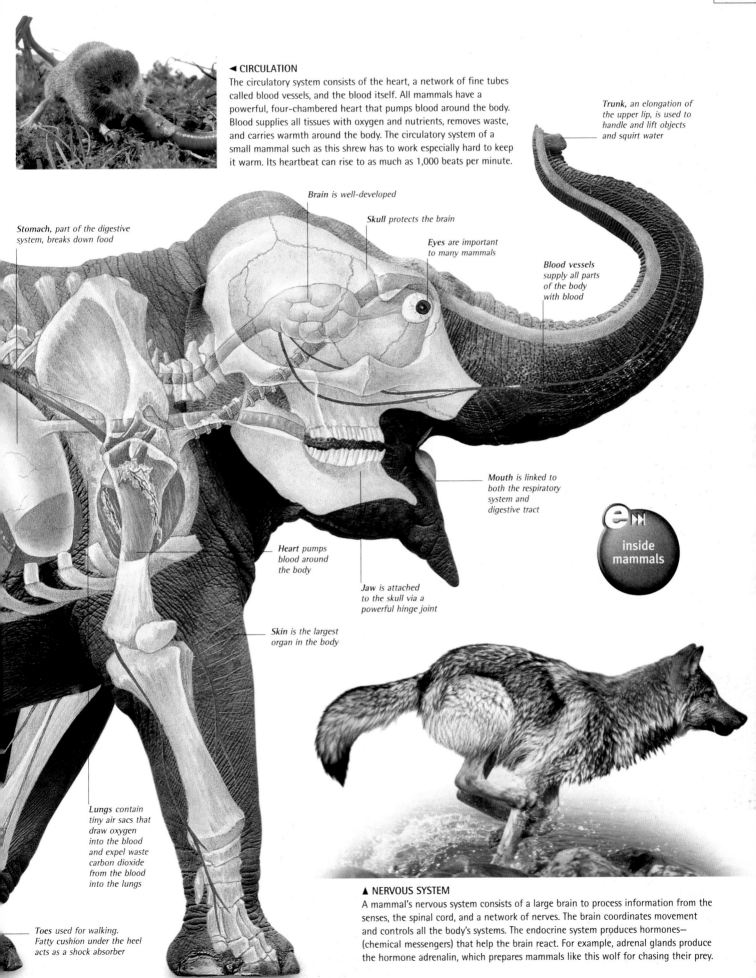

◄ CIRCULATION

The circulatory system consists of the heart, a network of fine tubes called blood vessels, and the blood itself. All mammals have a powerful, four-chambered heart that pumps blood around the body. Blood supplies all tissues with oxygen and nutrients, removes waste, and carries warmth around the body. The circulatory system of a small mammal such as this shrew has to work especially hard to keep it warm. Its heartbeat can rise to as much as 1,000 beats per minute.

Trunk, an elongation of the upper lip, is used to handle and lift objects and squirt water

Brain is well-developed

Skull protects the brain

Eyes are important to many mammals

Stomach, part of the digestive system, breaks down food

Blood vessels supply all parts of the body with blood

Mouth is linked to both the respiratory system and digestive tract

Heart pumps blood around the body

inside mammals

Jaw is attached to the skull via a powerful hinge joint

Skin is the largest organ in the body

Lungs contain tiny air sacs that draw oxygen into the blood and expel waste carbon dioxide from the blood into the lungs

Toes used for walking. Fatty cushion under the heel acts as a shock absorber

▲ NERVOUS SYSTEM

A mammal's nervous system consists of a large brain to process information from the senses, the spinal cord, and a network of nerves. The brain coordinates movement and controls all the body's systems. The endocrine system produces hormones—(chemical messengers) that help the brain react. For example, adrenal glands produce the hormone adrenalin, which prepares mammals like this wolf for chasing their prey.

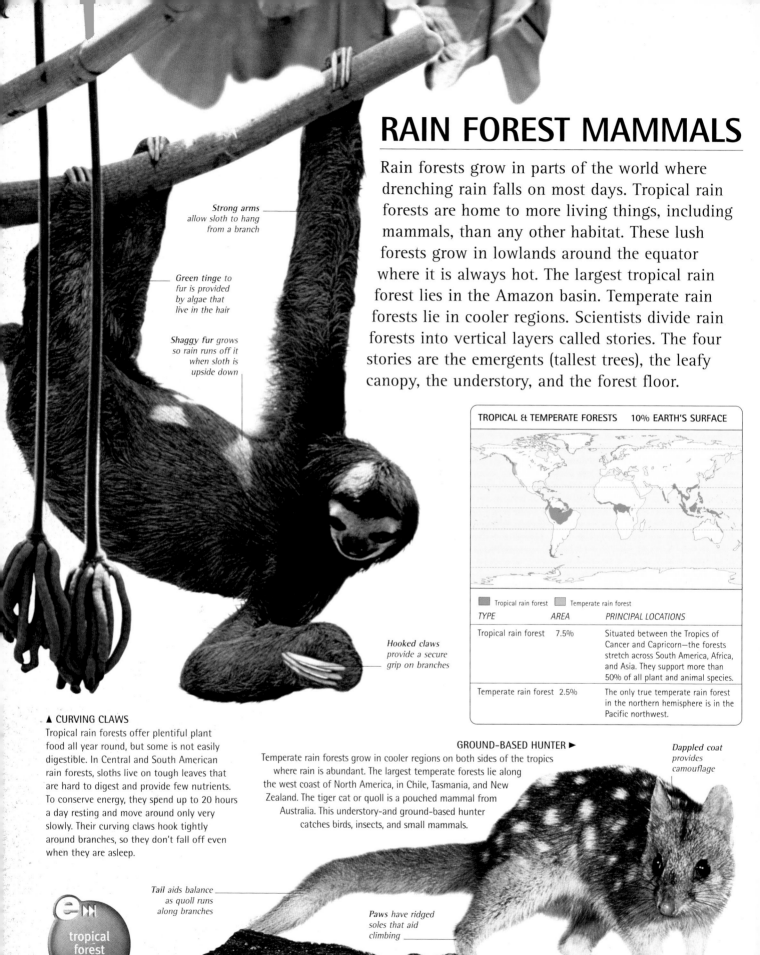

RAIN FOREST MAMMALS

Rain forests grow in parts of the world where drenching rain falls on most days. Tropical rain forests are home to more living things, including mammals, than any other habitat. These lush forests grow in lowlands around the equator where it is always hot. The largest tropical rain forest lies in the Amazon basin. Temperate rain forests lie in cooler regions. Scientists divide rain forests into vertical layers called stories. The four stories are the emergents (tallest trees), the leafy canopy, the understory, and the forest floor.

Strong arms allow sloth to hang from a branch

Green tinge to fur is provided by algae that live in the hair

Shaggy fur grows so rain runs off it when sloth is upside down

Hooked claws provide a secure grip on branches

TROPICAL & TEMPERATE FORESTS   10% EARTH'S SURFACE

◼ Tropical rain forest   ◻ Temperate rain forest

TYPE	AREA	PRINCIPAL LOCATIONS
Tropical rain forest	7.5%	Situated between the Tropics of Cancer and Capricorn—the forests stretch across South America, Africa, and Asia. They support more than 50% of all plant and animal species.
Temperate rain forest	2.5%	The only true temperate rain forest in the northern hemisphere is in the Pacific northwest.

▲ CURVING CLAWS
Tropical rain forests offer plentiful plant food all year round, but some is not easily digestible. In Central and South American rain forests, sloths live on tough leaves that are hard to digest and provide few nutrients. To conserve energy, they spend up to 20 hours a day resting and move around only very slowly. Their curving claws hook tightly around branches, so they don't fall off even when they are asleep.

GROUND-BASED HUNTER ▶
Temperate rain forests grow in cooler regions on both sides of the tropics where rain is abundant. The largest temperate forests lie along the west coast of North America, in Chile, Tasmania, and New Zealand. The tiger cat or quoll is a pouched mammal from Australia. This understory-and ground-based hunter catches birds, insects, and small mammals.

Dappled coat provides camouflage

Tail aids balance as quoll runs along branches

Paws have ridged soles that aid climbing

e ▶▶
tropical forest

Gibbon's muscular arms are longer than its legs

◄ CANOPY BY DAY

In tropical rain forests, trees soar over 165 ft (50 m) tall. High above ground, they spread their leaves to form a dense mat of foliage some 65 ft (20 m) deep. Most forest animals, including these white-faced gibbons, inhabit this wet, sunlit layer where food is abundant. Gibbons are skilled climbers and leapers. They get around by swinging from hand to hand, in a form of movement called brachiation.

Tail can grip branches

▲ CANOPY AT NIGHT

At night, a different set of mammals becomes active in tropical rain forests. Having a day and a night shift means that fewer animals are searching for food at any given time. In the Amazon rain forest, kinkajous spend the hours of daylight asleep in hollow trees. At night they emerge to search for fruit and insects. The long, prehensile (gripping) tail acts as a fifth limb, keeping the mammals safe as they move from tree to tree.

◄ UNDERSTORY BY DAY

Below the canopy, the understory layer is made up of shorter trees and saplings. The dense leaves above screen out most of the light and moisture, so plant food is scarcer here. In African rain forests, mandrills spend their day on the ground searching for fruit, eggs, and, occasionally, small animals. They climb into the understory at night to seek shelter from predators. These primates live in groups of about 20 mammals.

Large eyes are able to see well in very dim light

UNDERSTORY AT NIGHT ►

The understory is a dark place at night, lit only by faint glimmers of moonlight and perhaps the glow of fireflies. Nocturnal mammals must have a means of locating their food in very dim light. In the dense forests of Borneo, Southeast Asia, tarsiers detect their insect prey using keen vision, hearing, and smell. Sharp claws and toe pads grip branches as the little primate leaps through the understory, snatching at flying prey.

Long black tongue wrenches foliage from trees

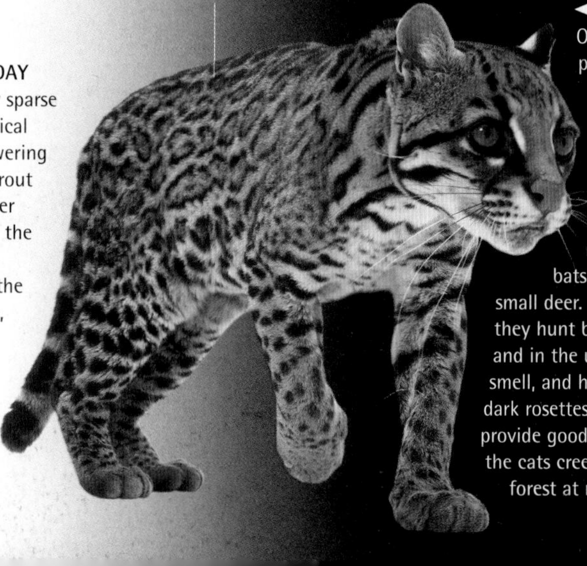

Markings differ between individuals

◄ FOREST FLOOR BY DAY

Vegetation is relatively sparse at ground level in tropical rain forests. Ferns, flowering plants, and saplings sprout in the thin soil wherever light filters through to the forest floor. In Central Africa, okapis wander the forest alone or in pairs, reaching up to browse the foliage. These large but wary mammals, related to giraffes, were not identified until 1901.

◄ FLOOR AT NIGHT

Ocelots are nocturnal predators of Central and South American rain forests. These stealthy hunters seek a wide range of prey, including birds, reptiles, and mammals such as bats, rodents, and even small deer. Skilled climbers, they hunt both on the ground and in the understory using sight, smell, and hearing. The dark rosettes on their skin provide good camouflage as the cats creep through the forest at night.

WOODLAND MAMMALS

Temperate woodlands and conifer forests contain fewer species than tropical rain forests, but are still rich in mammals. Conditions here vary far more than in the tropics, with warm or cool summers and cold winters. Most trees of temperate woodlands are deciduous—they shed their leaves in the fall and grow fresh ones in spring. Mammals rear their young in leafy, food-rich woods in summer. Conditions are harsher in winter. In the northern hemisphere, temperate woodlands make way for cold conifer forests where trees keep their leaves in winter, providing shelter for mammals. Woodlands and conifer forests can be divided into vertical layers called storys.

▲ BOAR ROOTING IN THE LEAF LITTER
In temperate woodlands, leaves shed by deciduous trees rot on the ground to form a rich compost that fuels plant growth. Trees and shrubs produce nuts and berries in the fall, feeding mammals such as badgers, squirrels, and wild boars like this one. In European and Asian woodlands, boars use their sensitive snouts to snuffle out roots, nuts, and fungi hidden in the leaf litter. Their sharp hooves dig up food below ground.

CONIFEROUS AND TEMPERATE	27% EARTH'S SURFACE	

TYPE	AREA	PRINCIPAL LOCATIONS
Coniferous	17%	Canada, Alaska, Scandinavia, Siberia
Temperate	10%	N America, Europe, China

Coniferous   Temperate

Stripes on head and gray upper body provide camouflage in dim light

BADGER HUNTING FOR FOOD ▶
In winter, woodlands bare of leaves offer little shelter for mammals. In Europe, Asia, and North America, badgers retreat to underground dens, called setts, to wait out the worst weather. These burrow networks can stretch for 65 ft (20 m) below ground. Badgers keep to their setts by day. At night they emerge to search for a variety of food, including fruit, insects, frogs, lizards, and small mammals.

Strong claws dig for worms

◀ WETLAND MOOSE
A vast belt of coniferous forest called the taiga rings the northern hemisphere between 45° and 65° north. These cold, damp forests hold millions of lakes and bogs. Moose, like this one, live in the wetlands. In summer they wade into the water to graze on floating plants and escape biting insects. Moose are the world's largest deer, with males weighing up to 1,000 lbs (450 kg).

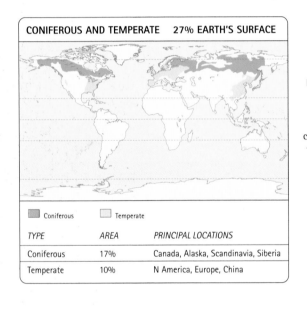

FORAGING IN THE UNDERSTORY ▶

The understory layer of temperate woodlands is made up of tall shrubs, saplings, and the trunks of mature trees. Bears, like these Asiatic black bears, divide their time between the understory and the forest floor. Like most bears, their diet is varied, including buds, leaves, insects, berries, and acorns, depending on the season. Strong claws and powerful limbs help these thickset mammals to shin up trees.

woodland

▲ CANOPY CLIMBER

The trees of temperate woodlands rarely grow more than 100 ft (30 m) tall. The leafy canopy is less dense than in tropical forests, so more light reaches the forest floor. Pine martens, like this one, are predators of temperate woodlands and northern conifer forests, pursuing beetles, rodents, birds, and also eating fruit. These lithe, slender mammals are at home in the treetops, but catch most of their food on the ground.

Large eyes give excellent vision and help squirrel judge distances

Fur is thick and woolly and provides insulation in snowy weather

Long tail helps squirrel balance

◀ ARBOREAL ACROBAT
Many mammals of temperate woodlands climb well, but none are more agile than squirrels. These graceful rodents build a nest called a drey high in the fork of a tree or in a hole in the trunk. Sharp, curving claws grip the bark as the squirrel leaps between branches or runs headlong up and down the trunk. In the fall, gray squirrels are busy burying acorns for the lean winter months. Forgotten nuts may sprout into young trees.

PANDAS

Giant pandas inhabit the deciduous forests of mountainous central China, where the understory is largely made of bamboo plants. These bears feed almost exclusively on bamboo, including shoots, leaves, and stems, although they also eat carrion, grubs, and eggs. A bony knob on the bear's wrist acts as a thumb, enabling the panda to grasp bamboo stems. This tough, stringy food provides little nourishment and is hard to digest, so pandas have to spend up to 18 hours a day eating.

The panda's black and white coloration may seem conspicuous, but actually breaks up the animal's outline, making it hard to spot in the bamboo thickets. These bears are solitary (live alone) and breed very slowly. As a result, fewer than 1,000 individuals are thought to survive in the wild.

GRASSLAND MAMMALS

The world's grasslands lie between moist regions where dense forests grow and dry areas occupied by desert. They split into temperate grasslands, such as the American prairies and Asian steppes, and tropical grasslands or savannahs. Grasslands support a wide range of mammals, including large, hoofed plant-eaters like antelope and bison, which live in herds, predators like lions and cheetahs, and scavengers such as jackals. Herbivores divide into browsers, which feed on scattered trees and shrubs, and grazers, which eat grass.

GRASSLANDS		17% EARTH'S SURFACE

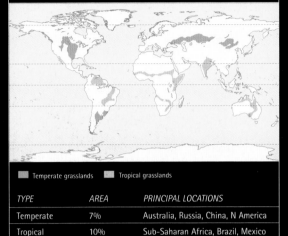

■ Temperate grasslands   ■ Tropical grasslands

TYPE	AREA	PRINCIPAL LOCATIONS
Temperate	7%	Australia, Russia, China, N America
Tropical	10%	Sub-Saharan Africa, Brazil, Mexico

Spine is very flexible, allowing cheetah to take large strides

e▸▸ grassland

MAMMAL GAIT

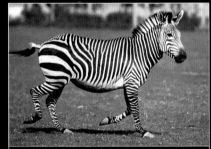

PACING
Speed is important to most grassland mammals. With little cover to hide behind, fast running often offers the best chance of either seizing prey or escaping enemies. Some mammals, such as this South American mara, pace. The mara is a type of cavy (South American rodent). When pacing, the front and back legs are coordinated. A pacing mammal moves the front and rear leg on the same side at once. Camels and elephants also pace.

TROTTING
When threatened, hoofed mammals such as zebras break into a trot (also called a diagonal gait), then accelerate into a canter and finally a gallop. A trotting mammal raises one foreleg and the opposite hind leg at the same time. Zebras' hooves have a hard protective outer layer with a pad of fat between it and the bones to act as a shock absorber when running at speed. Horses and dogs also trot.

◀ **FASTEST ON LAND**
On the plains of Africa, the cheetah is the sprint champion among land animals. It can race at up to 60 mph (100 kph) when trying to catch prey. However, it can only maintain this top speed for about 20 seconds before beginning to overheat. The cheetah's speed comes from its long, powerful legs and elastic spine, which flexes with every stride.

Sharp claws act like spikes on running shoes, gripping the ground

Long tail used for balance

Kangaroo leans forward with each bound

Two horns used for attacking

Black rhino can charge at up to 28 mph (45 kph)

Gray skin is darkened by wallowing in mud

▲ MOVING IN LEAPS AND BOUNDS
In the hot, dry Australian outback, grasslands are mixed with huge areas of dusty scrubland. Kangaroos survive by covering large distances, moving on two legs, not four. They bound along on their long, muscular back legs, which work like twin springboards. These mammals cruise comfortably at 12 mph (20 kph) and can flee from danger at up to 40 mph (60 kph). Kangaroos can cover 44 ft (14 m) in a single bound.

THREATS TO GRASSLAND MAMMALS

ROAMING THE PRAIRIES
Many grassland mammals are threatened by either loss of habitat, hunting, or both. Before Europeans colonized North America, vast herds of bison roamed the prairies. During the 19th century, as European settlers spread west, they slaughtered millions of bison, and the beasts almost died out. Small herds now thrive in parks and reserves.

SAVANNAH SPRINGBOK
African grasslands support the largest mammal herds on Earth. Herbivores such as these springbok antelope are safer in herds, since at any time, some animals will be watching for danger, while others graze. The springbok herds of southern Africa were once millions strong, but now the biggest herds number only 1,500 animals, as people encroach on their habitat.

MIGRATING WILDEBEEST
Like springbok, wildebeest also graze in large herds, sometimes in company with zebra. They migrate long distances across the African savannah in search of the fresh grass that springs up after rain, and give birth in February, when fresh grass is abundant. However, some traditional migration routes are now blocked by roads and other developments.

▲ LAND HEAVYWEIGHT
Africa's grasslands are home to the world's largest, heaviest land mammals: the African elephant and several species of rhinoceros, including this black rhino. Different rhino species feed on various grassland foods, with mouths adapted to their diet. The black rhino, a browser, uses its pointed upper lip to tear leaves from bushes. The white rhino has a square mouth suited to grazing. Rhinos are fairly timid but may break into a fast, lumbering charge when threatened.

DESERT DWELLERS

Most life cannot survive the extreme heat and dry soil of a desert habitat. Some mammals have adapted to survive the high temperatures and to find the water they need. During the day, smaller mammals burrow under sand or rock to hide from the heat. They emerge in the cool of the night to hunt for food and water. Large desert mammals cannot hide as easily and have to cope with the blazing sun. They often have pale fur, which reflects more of the sun's heat energy, keeping their bodies cooler.

DEATH VALLEY DAY ▲
California's Death Valley is the hottest, driest desert of the North American continent. Surface water from springs or scarce rainfall evaporates, leaving behind plant-killing salts.

200˚F

Ground sizzles at 190˚F (88˚C)   *Air temperature is 120˚F (49˚C) in shade*   *Saltwater pools reach 95˚F (35˚C)*

▲ RANGE OF TEMPERATURES OF DESERTS ROUND THE GLOBE
Desert temperatures around the world vary from the blistering heat of 190˚F (88˚C), as found in the Death Valley, to -4˚F (-20˚C), such as in the polar desert of the Dry Valleys, Antarctica.

◄ GROUND SQUIRREL

Tail shades the squirrel's body

Small-bodied mammals find it harder to regulate their body temperature than larger ones. Most small desert mammals solve the problem by sleeping through the day and hunting by night. The southern African ground squirrel has found a way to survive the heat during the day. It carries its bushy tail over its back, like a shady parasol.

CAMEL ADAPTATIONS

EYE SHIELDS
Dry deserts are dusty or sandy environments. Blown by the wind, sand and dust particles can damage sensitive eyes. Camels have two rows of long, thick eyelashes on each eyelid for protection. Underneath these normal eyelids, they also have a secret weapon: a third eyelid that wipes from side to side.

Eye protected from sand by extra eyelid and lashes

Hump stores energy from surplus food as a fatty deposit

Mouth is adapted to allow the camel to eat tough or thorny plants

Long legs hold the camel's body high above the hot desert surface

Flexible feet prevent sinking into soft sand

◄ SHIP OF THE DESERT
The Arabian camel or dromedary has one hump on its back. Bactrian camels from Central Asia have two humps. Both species have tall, narrow bodies to receive as little of the sun's heat as possible. The red blood cells of all camelids (members of the camel family) are structured so that when water is available, they can drink a large amount without bursting their cells.

NOSE AND MOUTH
Camel noses are designed to recycle the moisture that most mammals lose when they breathe out. Special muscles control the flexible nostril openings. The camel can pinch its nose shut in a sandstorm, protecting its lungs. The mouth is also specially adapted. A split upper lip helps the camel to handle prickly food.

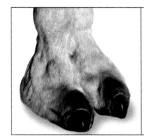

FEET
Camels' feet are wide and flexible, helping them walk easily over loose ground such as sand dunes. The leathery soles of the feet are tough but springy. Bones in the foot are separated from the sole by a pouch of fat. The pouch helps cushion pressure evenly across the sole. It also insulates the camel from the heat of the ground.

HUMPS
Camels stock up when they find a good food source. Spare calories are converted into fat, which is stored on the camel's back. This allows camels to travel long distances between feeding grounds, using the stored fat for energy. The chemical reaction for turning the fat into energy also creates water to cool the body.

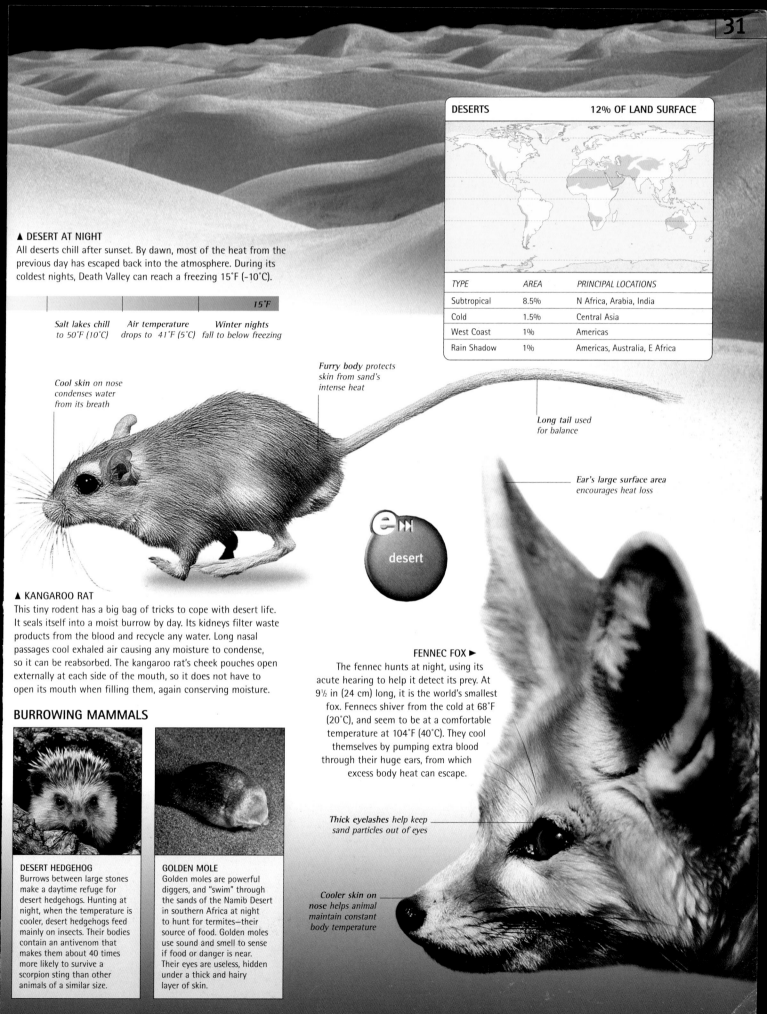

DESERTS — **12% OF LAND SURFACE**

TYPE	AREA	PRINCIPAL LOCATIONS
Subtropical	8.5%	N Africa, Arabia, India
Cold	1.5%	Central Asia
West Coast	1%	Americas
Rain Shadow	1%	Americas, Australia, E Africa

▲ DESERT AT NIGHT

All deserts chill after sunset. By dawn, most of the heat from the previous day has escaped back into the atmosphere. During its coldest nights, Death Valley can reach a freezing 15˚F (-10˚C).

15˚F

Salt lakes chill to 50˚F (10˚C) — *Air temperature drops to 41˚F (5˚C)* — *Winter nights fall to below freezing*

Cool skin on nose condenses water from its breath

Furry body protects skin from sand's intense heat

Long tail used for balance

Ear's large surface area encourages heat loss

desert

▲ KANGAROO RAT

This tiny rodent has a big bag of tricks to cope with desert life. It seals itself into a moist burrow by day. Its kidneys filter waste products from the blood and recycle any water. Long nasal passages cool exhaled air causing any moisture to condense, so it can be reabsorbed. The kangaroo rat's cheek pouches open externally at each side of the mouth, so it does not have to open its mouth when filling them, again conserving moisture.

FENNEC FOX ►

The fennec hunts at night, using its acute hearing to help it detect its prey. At 9½ in (24 cm) long, it is the world's smallest fox. Fennecs shiver from the cold at 68˚F (20˚C), and seem to be at a comfortable temperature at 104˚F (40˚C). They cool themselves by pumping extra blood through their huge ears, from which excess body heat can escape.

Thick eyelashes help keep sand particles out of eyes

Cooler skin on nose helps animal maintain constant body temperature

BURROWING MAMMALS

DESERT HEDGEHOG
Burrows between large stones make a daytime refuge for desert hedgehogs. Hunting at night, when the temperature is cooler, desert hedgehogs feed mainly on insects. Their bodies contain an antivenom that makes them about 40 times more likely to survive a scorpion sting than other animals of a similar size.

GOLDEN MOLE
Golden moles are powerful diggers, and "swim" through the sands of the Namib Desert in southern Africa at night to hunt for termites—their source of food. Golden moles use sound and smell to sense if food or danger is near. Their eyes are useless, hidden under a thick and hairy layer of skin.

polar and mountain

◄ THICK FUR
Cold is the one of the main enemies of polar and mountain mammals. Like all mammals found on land in the Arctic, the polar bear has a thick, furry coat that provides insulation against freezing temperatures and howling winds. Polar bears spend much of their time either in the water or roaming the floating ice, hunting their main prey—seals. A layer of fat below the skin helps them maintain an even body temperature.

Furry feet help polar bear retain heat

POLAR AND MOUNTAIN MAMMALS

The polar regions and mountains are some of the harshest places on Earth, with brief, cold summers and long, freezing winters. Darkness lasts for months on end in winter near the poles. The Arctic is relatively rich in mammals because the treeless lands there, called the tundra, are linked to warmer regions farther south. The vast, ice-smothered continent of Antarctica is too hostile for land-based mammal life, but seals and whales thrive in the seas. Mountain mammals must cope with thin air and intense sunlight as well as cold.

◄ FATTY BLUBBER
Marine mammals, including seals and whales, have even greater need of insulation than land mammals, because water draws body heat away more quickly than air. Whales and seals, such as this common seal, are less densely furred than land mammals, but keep warm with the help of a thick layer of fatty blubber just beneath the skin. In cold conditions, blood vessels running through the blubber contract (narrow) to help retain the body's heat.

Powerful front limbs are modified wrists and hands

▲ RUNNING ON SNOWSHOES
The snowshoe hare is named after its wide, furry feet, which act like snowshoes. As it speeds across the frozen landscape, wide feet help to spread its weight and prevent it from sinking into the soft snow. The snowshoe and its relative, the Arctic hare, have smaller ears and also shorter legs than hares found in warmer regions. These features help to cut down on the heat that is lost through limbs and ears.

VARIED CAMOUFLAGE

STOAT WITH WINTER COAT
The stoat is an Arctic predator that needs to stay camouflaged all year round. Its coat changes color with the seasons, allowing it to stalk prey such as lemmings throughout the year. In the fall the stoat grows a thick winter coat that is all white except for a black tail-tip. In this coat the animal is known as an ermine.

STOAT WITH SUMMER COAT
In spring, the ermine molts its thick winter fur. Its new, thinner coat is reddish-brown on top with creamy underparts, which blend in with the rocks and grass of the tundra once the snow has melted. Arctic and snowshoe hares, Arctic foxes, and weasels also vary in color, with gray or brown fur in summer and a white winter coat.

Tail *is 16 in (40 cm) long, and makes up over half of its body length*

Paws have hairy soles that reduce heat loss

POLAR AND MOUNTAIN

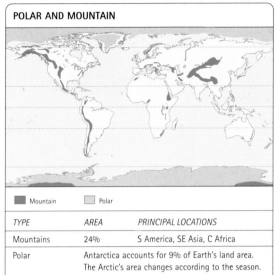

	Mountain		Polar

TYPE	AREA	PRINCIPAL LOCATIONS
Mountains	24%	S America, SE Asia, C Africa
Polar		Antarctica accounts for 9% of Earth's land area. The Arctic's area changes according to the season.

▲ SUITED TO THE COLD

The Arctic fox is able to remain active in conditions that would kill most mammals. Its white winter coat is twice as dense as its brown summer fur, with an outer layer of coarse hairs and fine underfur. The Arctic fox is well suited to the cold with its small, rounded, fur-lined ears that lose little heat, and paws with hairy soles that grip the ice. When sleeping, the fox wraps its long, bushy tail around its body to keep itself warm.

MOUNTAIN MAMMALS ▶

Yaks can survive at greater heights on mountains than almost any other animal— up to 20,000 ft (6,000 m) in the Himalayan mountains in Asia. The shaggy fur consists of coarse outer hairs that protect against wind and snow, and dense underfur that traps warm air next to the skin. High mountains offer several habitats in one, with boars, bears, and deer in forests on the lower slopes, and hardy goats and sheep on the grassy slopes above.

Curving horns provide defense against enemies

Snow does not melt on a yak as it loses so little body heat through fur

Horns grow on both males and females

Outer hairs reach almost to the ground

▲ GRIPPING HOOVES

Hoofed mammals, like this barbary sheep have hooves with hard edges and soft central soles that act like a suction cup, gripping onto steep, rocky surfaces. Callouses on their knees protect them from injury when lying down. Most mountain mammals have a large heart and lungs, which help them to cope with living at high altitude where the air is low in oxygen.

MARINE MAMMALS

Mammals evolved from reptiles on land, but some groups later returned to the water, where they adapted to an aquatic lifestyle. Three main groups of mammal are found in the oceans. They are pinnipeds (seals), cetaceans (whales, dolphins, and porpoises), and sirenians (manatees and dugongs). Both cetaceans and sirenians are purely aquatic, even giving birth in the water. The seal family includes sea lions and walruses. These mammals spend much of their life at sea, but come ashore to rest, breed, and give birth to their young.

marine

Whale's tail is divided into two halves, called flukes

▲ THE WHALE FAMILY

Whales resemble fish more closely than any other mammals. Their hind limbs have disappeared to create a sleek shape, while their front limbs have evolved into flippers used for steering. Unlike a fish's tail, the whale's notched tail is horizontally aligned. As the whale flexes its spine, its tail moves up and down to push the whale forward. Almost hairless, a thick layer of blubber helps the whale maintain an even body temperature.

Powerful front limbs used for propulsion

Webbed hind feet used to steer

Torpedo-shaped body slips easily through water

THE SEAL FAMILY ▲

The word pinniped means fin-footed. Seals' feet have evolved into flippers that push strongly against the water, while their bodies are compact and streamlined. Pinnipeds divide into three groups: true or earless seals; eared seals such as fur seals and these sea lions; and the walrus. In fact, all seals have ears, but "earless" seals lack outer earflaps. True seals use their hind limbs to propel themselves through the water, while eared seals use their front flippers. Sea lions and other eared seals are agile on land.

▲ TOOTHED WHALES

Cetaceans divide into two groups: toothed and baleen. Toothed cetaceans are by far the largest group, making up 90 percent of all cetaceans. This group includes sperm, beaked, and white whales, river dolphins, porpoises, and dolphins. This orca (killer whale) belongs to the group of dolphins. All toothed whales are meat-eaters, feeding on prey such as squid, fish, and shellfish, which they seize in their teeth. Orcas have powerful jaws lined with backward-pointing teeth.

▲ BALEEN WHALES

Baleen whales do not have teeth. They are named after the long, fringed plates of horny baleen that hang from their upper jaw. The baleen acts like a giant comb to sieve small creatures, such as krill, from the water. When the feeding whale takes a mouthful of food-rich water, the water is forced out over the baleen, leaving the prey behind. Baleen whales include the gray whale, right whales, and rorquals such as the blue whale, and the humpback whale, which is shown above.

RESPIRATION

SPOUTING

Like all mammals, whales and seals breathe air and have lungs. They have to return to the surface to breathe. A whale's blowhole (nostril) is on top of its head. After a dive, the whale surfaces and spouts a column of stale air and water vapor high in the air. When the sea is frozen, seals make breathing holes in the ice.

HUMAN WITH AQUALUNG

Whales are able to store oxygen in their muscles to remain under water for long periods. Most humans can hold their breath for less than two minutes. Humans must take an air supply with them when they explore the ocean depths. A wet suit acts like the hair of a fur seal, trapping a layer of warmer water next to the skin.

▼ WALRUS

The walrus is different enough from all other pinnipeds to be placed in its own group. This mammal is found only in the Arctic. One of the main characteristics that sets it apart are the long tusks, which both males and females possess. These are used to stir up the seabed for shellfish prey, and also help these large beasts to haul out or come ashore on ice. Males also use their tusks as weapons when fighting. The male walrus is the world's largest pinniped, weighing up to 3,000 lbs (1,360 kg). Half of its body weight is blubber.

Long hairs on muzzle form a bristly moustache

Reddish skin is covered with coarse hairs

Hind limbs can tuck under body to aid movement on land

Tough hide is creased into deep folds

Front flippers are used to steer when swimming

FRESHWATER MAMMALS

Freshwater habitats such as lakes, rivers, streams, and swamps are home to a variety of mammals, including voles, shrews, manatees, hippopotamuses, and river dolphins. Manatees and river dolphins are the only mammals here that are entirely water-dwelling. Lacking hind limbs, they never come ashore and their bodies are very different from those of land mammals. Other freshwater species dwell partly on the land and take to the water mostly to find food and escape from enemies. Adaptations (features) that suit various species to a watery lifestyle include thick hair, webbed feet, and a muscular tail.

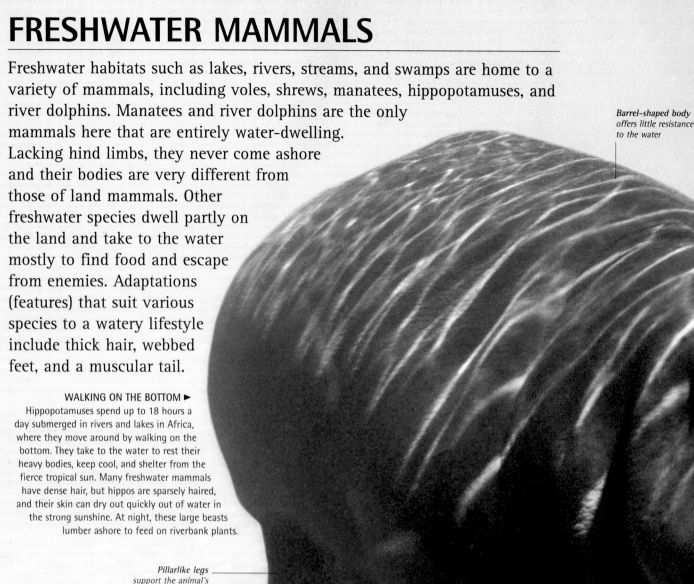

Barrel-shaped body offers little resistance to the water

WALKING ON THE BOTTOM ▶

Hippopotamuses spend up to 18 hours a day submerged in rivers and lakes in Africa, where they move around by walking on the bottom. They take to the water to rest their heavy bodies, keep cool, and shelter from the fierce tropical sun. Many freshwater mammals have dense hair, but hippos are sparsely haired, and their skin can dry out quickly out of water in the strong sunshine. At night, these large beasts lumber ashore to feed on riverbank plants.

Pillarlike legs support the animal's weight when on land

Water supports hippo's weight while it is submerged

DIVING FOR FOOD

Most shrews live on land, but several take to the water to escape predators and find food. They make repeated dives in search of small fish and underwater invertebrates, returning to land briefly to shake themselves dry. These little creatures need plenty of food to keep warm in the water. Some water shrews need to eat their own body weight in food every day. The silky fur is water-repellent. A fringe of stiff hairs along the edges of their feet and tail aids swimming and diving. This allows the very smallest shrews to run across the water surface for short distances, buoyed up by surface tension.

◄ MASTER BUILDERS
Beavers are largish aquatic rodents that inhabit rivers and lakes in Europe and North America. They build stick dams across rivers to make an artificial lake in which to build their home. A dense furry coat made up of coarse outer hairs and fine underfur keeps them warm both in and out of the water. However, in the 18th and 19th centuries, beaver fur was highly prized for making warm outer clothing. Millions of these mammals were killed by fur trappers.

BEAVER DAM ►
Beavers are among the few animals able to make major changes to their environment. Most beavers use sticks to construct a dam across a river. This creates a calm pool behind it, in which they construct their nest, called a lodge. Beavers gnaw through branches and saplings and then pile them high to dam the river.

Dam made of sticks positioned by beavers

Broad snout has touch-sensitive bristles

SUITED TO THE WATER

MANATEE
Manatees are gentle creatures that are found in rivers and also coastal waters in the tropics. These large mammals have plump bodies and powerful front limbs that are used as paddles. The broad, flattened tail is horizontally aligned like that of a whale. It sweeps up and down to push the animal forward.

DUCK-BILLED PLATYPUS
Duck-billed platypuses dwell by streams and rivers in Eastern Australia. They dive down to hunt aquatic creatures, including insects, shellfish, frogs, and worms. Awkward on land, the platypus is swift and graceful in the water. Its webbed feet and flat tail provide propulsion, while the soft, plushy fur repels water.

BEAVER
Webbed feet, a sleek, streamlined shape, and a flattened tail all help beavers move efficiently in water. The broad, scaly tail is mainly used as a rudder. The beaver paddles with its hind feet, keeping its front limbs tightly against its body for streamlining. When diving, its ears and nostrils close over to stop water from entering.

OTTER
Like other members of the weasel family, otters have long, slender bodies and small, doglike heads. These meat-eaters are energetic hunters and pursue prey such as fish, voles, crabs, frogs, and snails underwater. Webbed hind feet are used for swimming, while its clawed front feet grasp and hold slippery prey.

◄ SURFACING TO BREATHE
Hippos can spend around five minutes underwater before surfacing to breathe. As with many freshwater mammals, the eyes, ears, and nostrils are on the top of the head. This allows the hippo to breathe with just the upper part of the head above the surface.

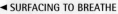

freshwater

BATS AND GLIDERS

Bats are the only mammals capable of powered flight. This allows them to colonize remote oceanic islands, such as New Zealand, not reached by other wild mammals. Bats are generally nocturnal, resting by day and seeking food at night. While bats are the only true flyers, a number of other mammals are able to glide though the air by spreading flaps of skin to act as a parachute.

◄ BATS IN FLIGHT
Flying enables bats to move from place to place, escape predators, and find food. The majority of bats catch their prey, in the form of flying insects, on the wing. Bats are extremely agile in the air, being able to twist, turn, and pass through narrow gaps. Flying uses up a lot of energy so bats save energy while resting by letting their body temperature drop.

Skin around nostrils is horseshoe-shaped giving bat its name

MICROBATS AND MEGABATS ▲
Bats vary considerably in size, ranging from large flying foxes with wings 5 ft (1.5 m) wide, to tiny hog-nosed bats the size of bumblebees. The bat order, Chiroptera, divides into two main groups: megabats or Old World fruit bats, and microbats. The group of microbats contains more than 80 percent of all bats, including horseshoe bats like this. Most microbats eat flying insects.

Furry flaps increase air resistance

Network of nerves and blood vessels runs through the wing

◄ CLOSE UP
A bat's wings consist of a double layer of skin stretched over the arm and leg bones and attached to the sides of the body. The hand and finger bones provide the framework. The name of the bat order, Chiroptera, means hand-wing. Muscles in the chest and upper arm sweep the wing down and forward, while back muscles pull it up again.

Tail may be used to brake and

◄ SUGAR GLIDER
Sugar gliders of Australian forests have furry flaps of skin running down the sides of their bodies, between their front and hind limbs. As they leap from a high perch, they stretch their limbs wide. The flaps slow their fall, so they swoop gently downward. However, they cannot fly. Flying lemurs (colugos), phalangers, and flying squirrels also glide using similar flaps.

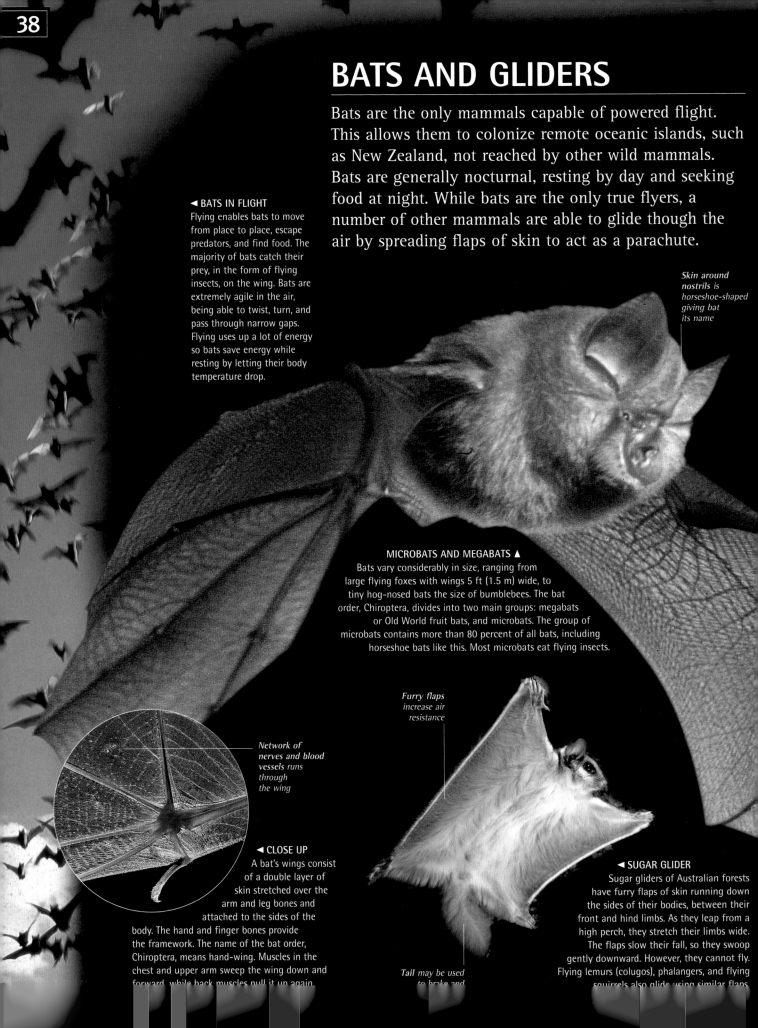

USING SENSES

KEEN HEARING
Various types of bats locate their food mainly through hearing, scent, or vision. The size of features such as eyes, ears, and noses reflects which senses are most important. Bats that use their keen hearing and the system of echolocation to find food, such as this common long-eared bat, are likely to have large ears.

SENSE OF SMELL
Neotropical fruit bats use their keen sense of smell and also sight to locate the fruit and nectar on which they feed. The spear-shaped noseflap is thought to deflect sounds toward the ears. This species also has a flap, called the tragus in front of its ear openings that is also thought to make its hearing more acute.

LARGE EYES
The phrase "blind as a bat" is not accurate. All bats have eyes and some see well. Megabats (or flying foxes) also feed on fruit and nectar. The large eyes of this night-active species make the most of gleams of light as it looks for food. Like its namesake, the fox, it also possesses an excellent sense of smell.

Wings fold by sides when not in use

Fur provides warmth

bats

BAT ROOSTS ▲
Bats pass the daylight hours resting in roosting sites such as caves, attics, and hollow trees. In cold climates, bats save energy in winter by hibernating in their roosts. Their clawed hind feet cling to the perch as they hang upside down with folded wings. The best roosting sites contain more than a million bats packed tightly together. At night when the bats leave to seek food, the air is filled with beating wings.

Wings can hover when sipping nectar

Bones are delicate and lightweight for flying

NECTAR FEEDER ▶
Most bats are insectivorous (feed on insects), but others eat rodents, frogs, and lizards, while fishing bats hook fish from pools. Vampire bats feed on blood. Megabats and some microbats, such as this common long-tongued bat, feed on plants, including fruit, flowers, pollen, and nectar. While sipping nectar, bats transfer pollen from one flower to another, fertilizing the plant.

Two layers of skin envelop the finger bones to form the wing

Bat's long tongue reaches nectar deep inside flowers

Feet are clawed to aid roosting

Flowers fertilized by bats open at night

SIGHT AND HEARING

For mammals, keen senses are vital for survival. Mammals use their senses to track down their food and to communicate with their own kind. Even more importantly, their senses work as an early warning system, giving them a chance to escape before danger strikes. Mammals have five main senses: sight, hearing, smell, taste, and touch. For some, smell is the most important sense, but for others sight and hearing are at the top of the list. Over millions of years, mammals have developed specialized eyes and ears to suit their ways of life.

◄ ALL-AROUND VISION
Unlike our eyes, a rabbit's eyes are on the sides of its head, and they face in opposite directions. As a result, the rabbit can see all around without having to move its head. Rabbits often feed out in the open, and their all-around vision helps them to spot predators before they have a chance to attack. Rabbits also have superb hearing—this protects them when they feed after dark.

Wide field of view does not overlap

Overlapping fields of view allow a bushbaby to see in 3-D

◄ FORWARD FACING EYES
Like most primates, this bushbaby has large forward-facing eyes. Whenever it looks at anything, its eyes see the same scene, but from two slightly different points of view. This is called binocular vision. It allows bushbabies to see depth and to judge distances accurately—a vital skill for an animal that lives in trees and that hunts insects after dark. Humans also have binocular vision. We use it whenever we move, and particularly when we play sports.

INSIDE THE HUMAN EYE

The human eye works by gathering light. The curved surface of the cornea and the lens help focus the light on the retina producing an upside down image and triggering photoreceptors, or light-sensitive nerves. Nerve impulses are sent via the optic nerve to the brain where the image is turned the right way up, and information, such as size, distance, and color are assessed. In other mammals, the quality of the image depends on the position of the eyes, the number of photoreceptors on the retina, and whether or not they see in color.

Retina

Cornea

Light rays from image enter the eye

Elastic lens changes shape to make focus sharp

◄ SHINING EYES
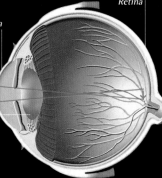
After dark, this jaguar's eyes seem to light up with an eerie yellow glow. The glow is called eyeshine, and is produced by a shiny layer, called the tapetum lucidum, which lies at the back of the eye. The tapetum lucidum reflects any incoming light back through the eye, enabling the jaguar to see in low-light conditions. Eyeshine is common in nocturnal predators, such as cats and foxes. It is often yellow, but it can also be red or green.

RODENT 1,000–100,000 HZ
Different mammals can sense different pitches, or frequencies, of sound. Rodents can hear sounds with a pitch of up to 100,000 Hz (waves per second), which is far too high for us to hear. However, their ears cannot pick up low sounds. To them, most of the keys on a piano would seem to make no sound at all.

SEALS 200–55,000 HZ
Unlike rodents, a seal's ears work equally well in water and in air. Sound travels farther in water than in air, and seals use it to keep in touch with each other as they feed. Seals are good at hearing high-pitched sounds, and some kinds may be able to use echolocation, although this has not yet been proved.

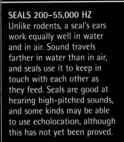

DOLPHINS 70–150,000 HZ
Dolphins have excellent hearing, and use echolocation to find their food. Like bats, they use sounds with a very high pitch, because this gives the clearest echoes. Marine dolphins have quite good eyesight, but river dolphins are almost blind. They rely on echolocation to find their way through the muddy waters.

DOGS 40–46,000 HZ
Dogs can hear much higher sounds than we can. Wolves communicate by howling—an eerie sound that helps to gather the pack together before a hunt and whips them into a frenzy of excitement so that they are even more eager to chase and kill their prey. Foxes can pinpoint their rodent prey by sound alone.

HUMANS 20–20,000 HZ
Compared to many mammals, humans have a narrow hearing range. We are good at hearing deep sounds, but not so good with sounds that are high-pitched. Like all mammals, our hearing also changes as we grow up. Infants and children have very sensitive hearing, but in later life, high-pitched sounds become harder to hear.

ELEPHANTS 16–12,000 HZ
Elephants keep in touch by trumpeting, but they also make low, rumbling sounds that are too deep for us to hear. These "infrasound" calls can be heard by other elephants up to 2½ miles (4 km) away. Elephants cannot hear high-pitched sounds such as birds singing or chirping insects.

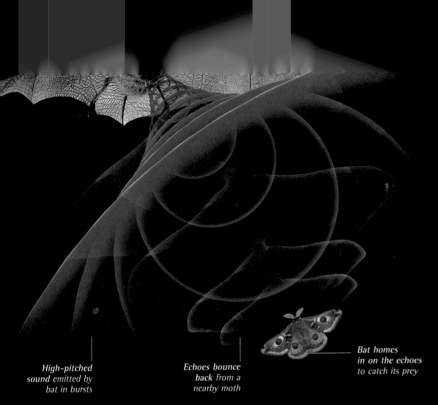

High-pitched sound emitted by bat in bursts

Echoes bounce back from a nearby moth

Bat homes in on the echoes to catch its prey

▲ ECHOLOCATION
Insect-eating bats can hunt in total darkness, using sound to pinpoint their prey. They produce pulses of high-pitched sound, which bounce off anything that is nearby. By listening for the echoes, a bat homes in on its target, and then snatches it up in its jaws. This way of using sound to "see" is called echolocation. Bats use echolocation to find their way into empty buildings, and also deep into caves. Their echolocation is amazingly precise, but it is not always foolproof. Moths sometimes jam a bat's signals by producing high-pitched sounds of their own.

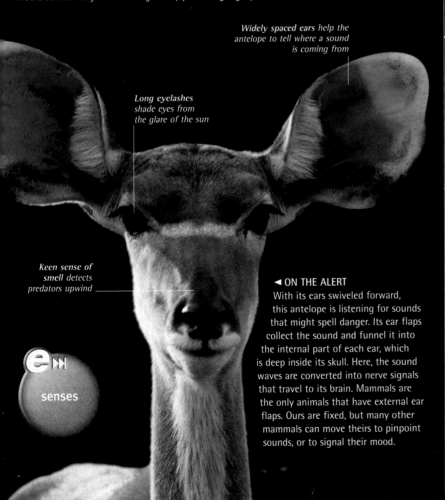

Widely spaced ears help the antelope to tell where a sound is coming from

Long eyelashes shade eyes from the glare of the sun

Keen sense of smell detects predators upwind

◄ ON THE ALERT
With its ears swiveled forward, this antelope is listening for sounds that might spell danger. Its ear flaps collect the sound and funnel it into the internal part of each ear, which is deep inside its skull. Here, the sound waves are converted into nerve signals that travel to its brain. Mammals are the only animals that have external ear flaps. Ours are fixed, but many other mammals can move theirs to pinpoint sounds, or to signal their mood.

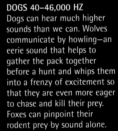

e ▸▸

senses

SMELL, TASTE, AND TOUCH

For humans, being able to smell is less important than being able to see or hear. But for wolves and many other predators, smell is the most important sense of all. It can guide a wolf pack to its prey across vast areas of open snow, and it can also work as an identity badge, and a way of signaling when an animal is ready to mate. Unlike smell, taste and touch work at close quarters. Mammals use taste to make sure that food is safe to eat, while touch enables mammals to judge widths, find food, and maintain hierachies in packs or herds.

◄ HOW SMELL WORKS

The outer part of a fox's nose leads to a cavity inside its skull. This cavity is filled with turbinal bones—paper-thin folds that are covered with cells bathed in mucus. When the fox breathes in, air flows past these folds and is warmed, moistened, and cleaned. The air then flows past nerves, called smell receptors, which detect different kinds of airborne chemicals. The receptors send signals to the fox's brain, and the fox uses the signals to recognize a scent.

Fleshy nose

Lip

Palate

Brain cavity

Sinuses are full of air

Nasal cavity with paper-thin turbinal bones

ON THE TRAIL ►

To a wolf, a scent trail is a mine of information. It can tell wolves where an animal went, how fast it was traveling, and how long ago it was on the move. By sniffing an animal's urine, they can often tell what sex it is, and whether or not it is in good health. For wolves, poor health is a promising sign, because it means they have a better chance of outrunning their prey.

MAMMAL NOSES

STAR-NOSED MOLE
Most moles have pointed snouts, but this North American species has a ring of 22 fleshy tentacles around its nostrils. It eats worms and insects and uses its tentacles to feel for food. Compared to other moles, it has a poor sense of smell, but a good sense of touch.

SHORT-NOSED ECHIDNA
Also known as the spiny anteater, this egg-laying mammal has a snout shaped like a pencil. It feeds on termites, ants, and worms, tracking down its food mainly by smell. Echidnas also use smell to find their way and sense danger. They have small eyes and their eyesight is poor.

PLATYPUS
The platypus's beak is a perfect implement for finding food in muddy water. It is very sensitive to touch, but it can also detect the faint electrical fields that surround living animals. This electrical sense enables the platypus to locate animals hidden at the bottom of ponds and streams.

TONGUES AND TASTE BUDS

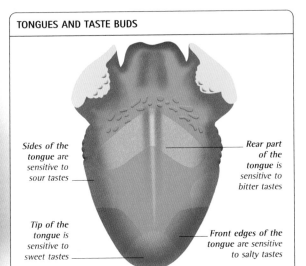

Sides of the tongue are sensitive to sour tastes

Rear part of the tongue is sensitive to bitter tastes

Tip of the tongue is sensitive to sweet tastes

Front edges of the tongue are sensitive to salty tastes

Humans can sense dozens of different smells, but we can only sense four basic tastes: sweet, sour, salty, and bitter. When we eat, these tastes are detected by taste buds on the surface of the tongue that send signals to the brain. Different parts of the tongue specialize in different tastes, although most taste buds can actually detect all four. On its own, taste is not enough to identify different kinds of food. To appreciate something's full flavor, we have to smell it as well.

CLEANING UP ▶

Carnivores, like this lioness, kill and eat fresh meat, which they swallow in chunks without chewing. They are therefore thought to have a poor sense of taste. Ungulates (grazing animals) that chew their food, sometimes for long periods, are thought to have a better sense of taste. Domestic horses develop a sweet tooth—they love carrots and peppermints, which they would not eat in the wild.

Long tongue washes muzzle after eating

NIMBLE FINGERS ▶

When raccoons feed, they often pick up their food in their paws. Like our fingers, a raccoon's paws are packed with pressure-sensitive nerves, enabling it to adjust its grip. Unlike smell and taste, touch works all over a mammal's body. Some body parts—such as whiskers—are highly sensitive to touch, helping mammals to move around safely in confined spaces, or after dark.

senses

Tail used for balance when climbing

Long, sensitive whiskers

◀ KEEPING IN CONTACT

Standing head to head, these two baby elephants are taking time off to play. When mammals are born, touch is often their most important sense, and it plays a key part in life as they grow up. Young elephants often touch each other with their trunks, while mothers use theirs to guide their young into the safety of the herd. Adult primates often groom each other. This form of touching helps to show an animal's rank in a social group.

Nose has a keen sense of smell

Raccoon's paws are highly sensitive to touch

FEEDING

Food is converted into energy that is used to maintain all of a mammal's bodily functions. A camel can go for days without eating, because it has a store of fat in its hump, but the smallest mammals—such as shrews—have to eat round the clock to survive. Many mammals have become specialized feeders. Herbivores eat plants, while carnivorous mammals feed on other animals. The least choosy eaters are omnivores, opportunists, and scavengers. They feed on a wide range of food, alive or dead.

FEEDING ON FRUIT ▶
This Japanese macaque is eating some fruit. Macaques feed mainly on plant food, and they help trees to spread by scattering their seeds, either in their dung or if seeds gets caught in their fur. But like most primates, they also try other foods as well. All macaques eat insects and birds' eggs as they forage among the trees. In Southeast Asia, macaques also forage along the shore, collecting crabs and other animals that have been stranded by the tide.

◀ EATING LEAVES
The koala has one of the most specialized diets in the mammal world. It eats the leathery leaves of eucalyptus trees, munching its way through about 1 lb (500 g) a day. Few other plant-eaters touch these leaves, because they contain strong smelling oils, but the koala's digestive system is specially adapted to break them down. This kind of diet is low in protein and in energy. Koalas make up for this by moving slowly, and by sleeping for up to 80 percent of the time.

Long tongue and pointed snout probe deep into flowers

NECTAR FEEDERS ▶
The tiny honey possum feeds on nectar and pollen from flowers. Nectar provides it with energy and water, while pollen gives it the protein it needs. Protein is particularly important for breeding females, because they need it to make milk for their young. This diet is only possible in places where plants flower all year round. In the honey possum's habitat, there are hundreds of species of shrubs, and many of them flower for months at a time.

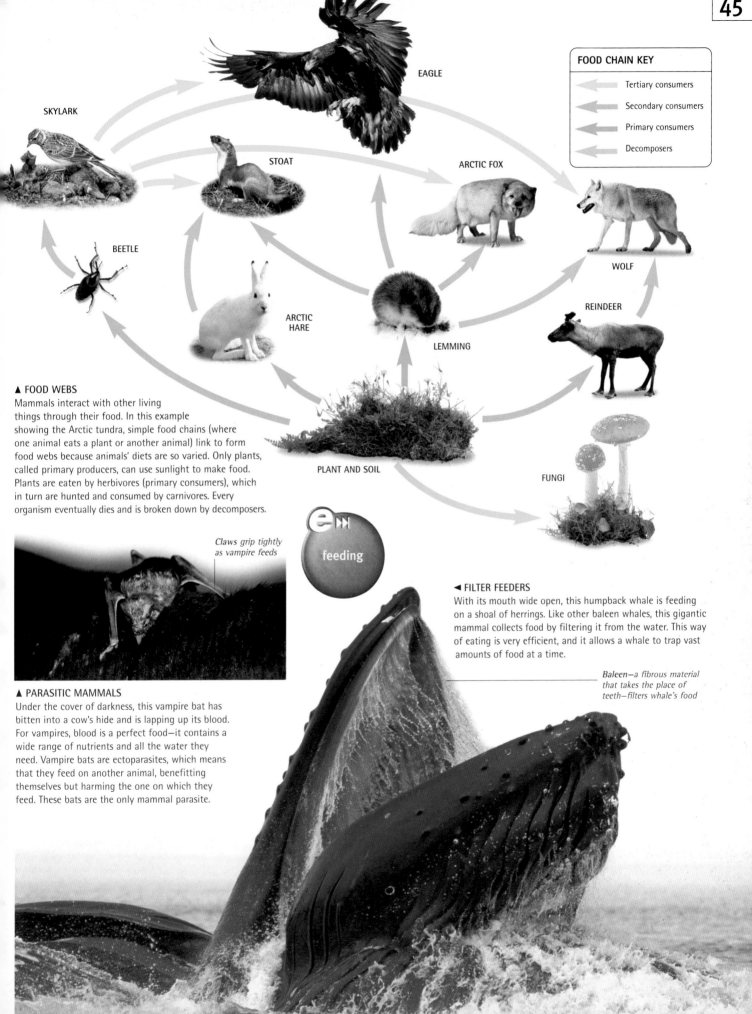

EAGLE

SKYLARK

STOAT

ARCTIC FOX

FOOD CHAIN KEY

Tertiary consumers

Secondary consumers

Primary consumers

Decomposers

WOLF

BEETLE

REINDEER

ARCTIC HARE

LEMMING

FUNGI

▲ FOOD WEBS

Mammals interact with other living things through their food. In this example showing the Arctic tundra, simple food chains (where one animal eats a plant or another animal) link to form food webs because animals' diets are so varied. Only plants, called primary producers, can use sunlight to make food. Plants are eaten by herbivores (primary consumers), which in turn are hunted and consumed by carnivores. Every organism eventually dies and is broken down by decomposers.

PLANT AND SOIL

Claws grip tightly as vampire feeds

feeding

◄ FILTER FEEDERS

With its mouth wide open, this humpback whale is feeding on a shoal of herrings. Like other baleen whales, this gigantic mammal collects food by filtering it from the water. This way of eating is very efficient, and it allows a whale to trap vast amounts of food at a time.

Baleen—a fibrous material that takes the place of teeth—filters whale's food

▲ PARASITIC MAMMALS

Under the cover of darkness, this vampire bat has bitten into a cow's hide and is lapping up its blood. For vampires, blood is a perfect food—it contains a wide range of nutrients and all the water they need. Vampire bats are ectoparasites, which means that they feed on another animal, benefitting themselves but harming the one on which they feed. These bats are the only mammal parasite.

CHISELERS AND GNAWERS

Rodents make up 40 percent of all the world's mammals. They are found everywhere except Antarctica—and where they have adapted to life in cities, they have increased to such numbers that they are considered a pest. Small rodents often breed quickly and have large litters, so their numbers increase rapidly. Rodents have incisor teeth that grow continuously to compensate for chiseling and gnawing, which wears teeth down. Rabbits and hares also have incisor teeth, which grow nonstop to counteract the silica in grass that wears them down. Chiselers and gnawers include some successful planteaters, as well as pests.

rodents

◄ LAGOMORPHS
Hares, rabbits, and pikas make up a group of mammals called lagomorphs. Lagomorphs are similar to rodents, but they have two pairs of incisor teeth in their upper jaw. Their second pair are small and peglike and sit immediately behind the larger pair. Lagomorphs are strict vegetarians—unlike many rodents—and they usually feed out in the open, often after dark.

Large incisors gnaw through tree trunks

SELF-SHARPENING TEETH

Lagomorphs and rodents chew with their front teeth, or incisors. Unlike human incisors, theirs are curved and keep growing. Their front surface is made of hard enamel, but their rear surface is made of a softer material, called dentine. When they gnaw, their incisors scrape together, which keeps them sharp. Their chewing teeth or molars are set far back in their jaws, giving them the strongest possible bite.

RABBIT SKULL

Upper jaw has two large incisors, and two small ones behind them

BEAVER SKULL

Incisors can be more than 1 in (3 cm) long

Large gap, or diastema, between incisors and molars

▲ FELLING TREES
After an hour or more of hard work, this beaver has gnawed through a tree. Beavers use trees to dam streams, making artificial lakes. The beavers live in the center of the lake, in a hollow island of branches and sticks, known as a lodge. The entrances to the lodge are underwater, so the beavers can come and go unseen, and they can also reach their submerged stores of food in winter when the lake is frozen.

DIGESTING FOOD

Leafy food is difficult to digest, because it contains a tough substance called cellulose that mammals cannot digest. Rodents and lagomorphs use special microbes that they store in a blind-ended pouch, called the cecum. When food enters the cecum, the microbes break down its cellulose, turning it into cellulase, which the animal can digest. Rabbits and hares often eat their own droppings once food has passed through their bodies. This gives them a second chance to digest it, getting more energy and nutrients.

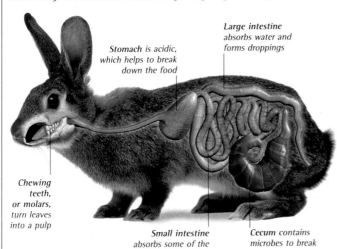

Stomach is acidic, which helps to break down the food

Large intestine absorbs water and forms droppings

Chewing teeth, or molars, turn leaves into a pulp

Small intestine absorbs some of the nutrients in food

Cecum contains microbes to break down cellulose

Paws pick up cereal grains

ADAPTABLE RODENTS ▶

The house mouse is one of the most widespread rodents, because it has adapted to life with humans in both towns and the countryside. Rats also live alongside humans, stealing food and sometimes spreading disease. They are also intelligent and learn not to eat poisoned foods, making them difficult to control. But not all rodents are this successful. Some species—such as the South American chinchilla—are endangered because they have been hunted for food or for their fur.

CARRYING FOOD

FILLING UP

The golden hamster has small paws, but it is an expert at carrying food. To do this, it uses a pair of elastic cheek pouches that it can fill up like grocery bags. Here, a hamster has found a collection of nuts. Using its teeth and its paws, it starts to collect food to take back to its home.

BACK TO THE BURROW

The hamster's cheek pouches reach back as far as its shoulders, and, being elastic, they stretch out so the hamster can take all the nuts on board. Although its pouches are full, its paws are still free, so it can move without the food getting in the way. Loaded up, the hamster heads straight back to its burrow.

UNPACKING

To unpack the food, the hamster tightens up its cheek pouches, and squeezes them with its paws. Once its pouches are empty, it arranges the food in its store, and then heads back to collect more. To carry larger pieces of food, such as roots and bulbs, the hamster holds them in its incisor teeth instead.

Tail used for balancing when jumping over rocky ground

◀ SURVIVING TOUGH TIMES

Mongolian gerbils come from the deserts of Central Asia, where summers are dry and hot, and winters cold. To survive in this kind of habitat, wild gerbils live in burrows, and they often store food underground. Each gerbil family needs more than 22 lb (10 kg) of seeds to feed them for several months. Like many desert rodents, gerbils can survive with very little water because they get the moisture they need from their food.

Large eyes can see in dim light

Sharp teeth bite through nut's hard casing

DEXTROUS PAWS ▶

Sitting on its haunches, this gray squirrel is using its front paws to hold a nut while it feeds. With pinecones, the squirrel's paws are even more agile, turning the cone around while the animal's teeth strip off the hard scales to get to the seeds. Many other rodents are just as nimble-fingered. They use their paws for all kinds of tasks, from running and climbing to grooming their fur. To burrow underground, they often use their teeth as well.

GRAZERS AND BROWSERS

Many mammals feed on plants, but hoofed mammals are specialists in this way of life. In size, they range from the tiny mouse deer, no bigger than a rabbit, to the tank-like white rhino, which can weigh over 3½ tons (3 metric tons). These grazers and browsers include zebras and antelopes, which form spectacular herds on grassy plains, and also many farm animals, such as cattle, sheep, goats, and pigs. Most of these animals are good runners, with long legs and compact feet, and all of them have unusual teeth and digestive systems to help them deal with their food.

Brown coat provides camouflage in dry grass

▲ GRAZERS

Grazing animals, such as zebras, feed almost exclusively on grass. Zebras have continually growing cheek teeth because the older, drier grasses on which they feed are abrasive (scratchy) and wear their teeth down. Other grazers, such as wildebeest, live alongside zebras but feed mainly on young grass shoots so that they are not in competition with the zebras for food.

▲ BROWSERS

Browsers feed on shrubs and trees. Browsers include goats, deer, some antelopes, and giraffes—the tallest browsers of all. Giraffes can stand 16 ft (5 m) high, and gather their food using thorn-proof lips and a long tongue. Others reach food in different ways. The black rhino has a mobile, hooked lip for collecting browse, whereas the gerenuk, a type of antelope, stands on its hind legs to reach its food.

LIFE ON THE MOVE ▲

Tilting over as it turns, a male impala chases a rival out of his breeding territory. These elegant antelopes live in grassland and open woodland, and they switch between grazing and browsing at different times of the year. Like most antelope, impala live in herds, and they have elaborate social behavior. Males mingle freely for most of the year, but they spar (fight) with each other when it is time to breed.

RUMINANT

Rumen contains microbes that break down cellulose

Colon

Small intestine

Passage of food (first time)

Passage of food (second time)

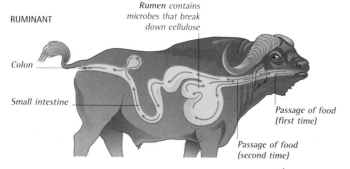

NONRUMINANT

Cecum Stomach

Colon

Passage of food

Small intestine

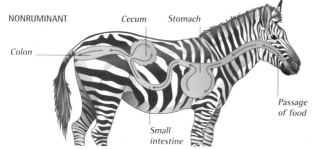

▲ DIGESTIVE SYSTEMS

Hoofed mammals have evolved two different kinds of digestive systems for breaking down plant food. Ruminants—such as buffalo and deer—have four stomach chambers. Grass is broken down by microbes in the largest chamber, called the rumen. After this, the animal regurgitates its food and chews it again, before it passes through the rest of its digestive system. Nonruminants have a simpler, but equally successful, digestive system with microbes in the cecum.

FOOD AND FEEDING

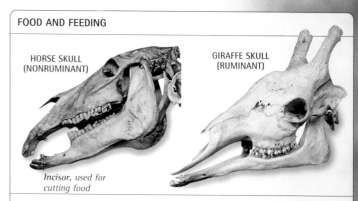

HORSE SKULL (NONRUMINANT)

GIRAFFE SKULL (RUMINANT)

Incisor, used for cutting food

Horses and zebras collect grass by biting it off with their incisor teeth. They then move the food with their tongues to the back of the mouth, where two rows of ridged molar teeth grind it up. Ruminants lack upper incisors and use their lips and tongues to gather food, which is then either nibbled off or pulled away. When they bite, their lower incisors press against a hard pad in the upper jaw, instead of against other teeth, enabling them to snip off foliage.

*Horns only found
on male impala*

*Hollow hairs help
to trap body heat*

▲ THE CAMEL FAMILY

With their thick fur, vicunas survive freezing nights high up in the Andes mountains. They belong to the camel family—a small group of hoofed mammals that includes llamas, and also camels themselves. These animals specialize in tough habitats. Vicunas live at altitudes of up to 16,000 ft (4,800 m), where the thin air makes it hard for most mammals to breathe. Camels can survive temperatures of 120°F (50°C) by day and 15°F (-10°C) at night.

▼ ANTLERS AND HORNS

At the height of the breeding season, mature male deer have impressive antlers, which they display to their rivals. Antlers are made of solid bone, and they grow afresh each year. At the end of the breeding season, they are shed. Almost immediately, a new pair starts to appear. Unlike antlers, horns last for life. They comprise a core of bone covered with a keratin (the same hard substance that forms hooves and hair) sheath. Animals with horns include cattle and antelopes.

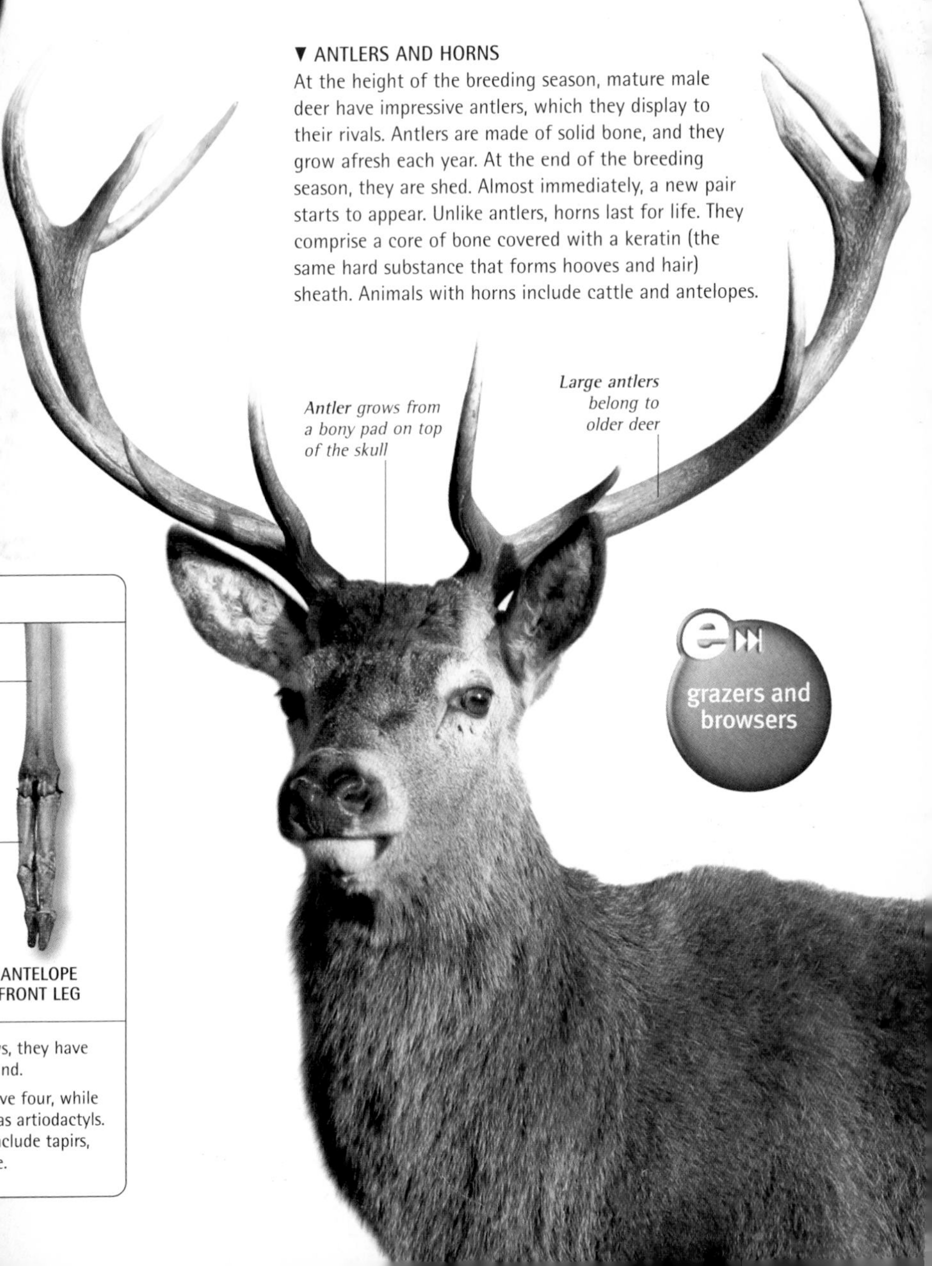

*Antler grows from
a bony pad on top
of the skull*

*Large antlers
belong to
older deer*

e ▶▶
grazers and browsers

*Long, slender legs
end in narrow toe-
toed hooves*

ODD AND EVEN TOES

*Fourth
toe does
not
reach
ground*

Slender leg bones

*Three
weight-
bearing
toes*

*Two toes
with narrow
hooves*

*Single (third)
toe*

TAPIR
FRONT LEG

HORSE
FRONT LEG

ANTELOPE
FRONT LEG

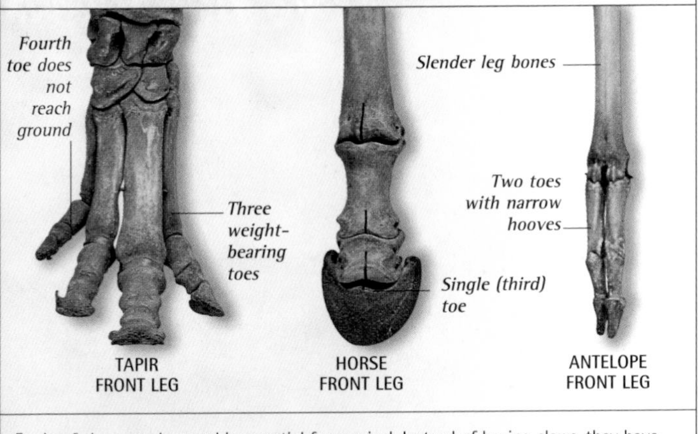

For hoofed mammals, speed is essential for survival. Instead of having claws, they have hooves—hard shock-resistant nails that help them to sprint across the ground.

Most hoofed mammals have an even number of toes. Pigs, for example, have four, while deer, antelopes, and cattle have two. Together, these mammals are known as artiodactyls. A smaller group, called perissodactyls, have an odd number of toes. They include tapirs, rhinos, and horses. Tapirs have three working toes. Horses have just one toe.

INSECT-EATERS

For many mammals, invertebrates are an essential source of food. Bats catch insects on the wing, while mammals known as insectivores hunt them on or in the ground. Insectivores include hedgehogs, shrews, and moles, as well as solenodons and tenrecs. Most of these animals are experts at finding invertebrates by smell or by touch. Insectivores are often small, but the biggest insect-eating mammals—aardvarks and anteaters—can weigh as much as an adult man. They have appetites to match, devouring thousands of ants or termites a day.

INSECT-EATERS' TEETH

Insect-eating animals come from several different branches of the mammal world. The shape of their teeth and skulls depends partly on their ancestry and partly on their diet. True insectivores—such as shrews and hedgehogs—have teeth that are small but sharp. Their prey can be almost as big as they are, so they need teeth for cutting it up. Giant insect-eaters, such as the aardvark, often have simple peglike teeth, or no teeth at all. They live on small termites and ants, and they usually swallow them whole. The long-beaked echidna—a monotreme—eats the same kind of food. It does not have teeth, but grinds up its food with hard plates at the back of its mouth.

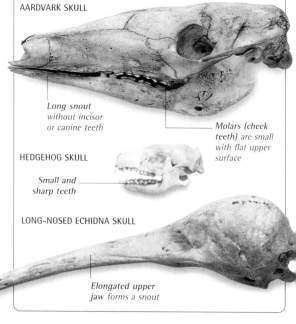

AARDVARK SKULL

Long snout without incisor or canine teeth

Molars (cheek teeth) are small with flat upper surface

HEDGEHOG SKULL

Small and sharp teeth

LONG-NOSED ECHIDNA SKULL

Elongated upper jaw forms a snout

insect eaters

▲ NIGHT PATROL

Using its sensitive nose, this hedgehog has tracked down a slug. Like many insectivores, hedgehogs are not fussy about their food. They eat all kinds of small animals, from slugs and snails to earthworms and beetles, and they also raid nests to get at eggs. A hedgehog is protected by sharp spines that cover its head and back. If it is threatened, it raises its spines, and then rolls up into a tight ball, protecting its underside and legs.

ATTACK FROM BELOW ▶

This Grant's golden mole has successfully ambushed a locust and is starting on its meal. Golden moles live in deserts and they move by "swimming" through sandy soil. They usually feed on termites, but if they sense a large insect moving on the surface, they attack it from below. Golden moles have tiny eyes, which are covered with skin, and strong front legs with picklike claws. They get their name from their fur, which has a metallic sheen.

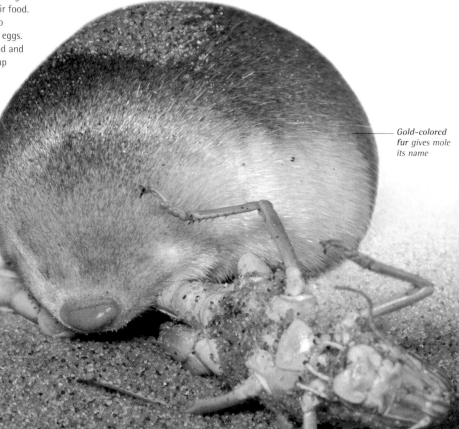

Gold-colored fur gives mole its name

OTHER INSECT-EATERS

SOLENODON
Solenodons are highly unusual insectivores that live only on the islands of Cuba and Hispaniola. About the size of a cat, they have soft, flexible snouts—ideal for probing into crevices, or for foraging among fallen leaves. Solenodons are good climbers, and have toxic saliva that helps them to kill their prey.

TENREC
The 30 species of tenrecs come from Africa and Madagascar. Like solendons, most live in tropical forests and get their food on the ground. Tenrecs have compact bodies and long snouts and a coat of coarse fur, sometimes interspersed with spines. The streaked tenrec, shown here, has spines up to 1¼ in (3 cm) long.

AARDVARK
Weighing up to 145 lb (65 kg), the African aardvark is the heaviest mammal that lives entirely on insects, and is one of the world's fastest diggers. It has large ears and a piglike snout, and it uses its powerful front claws to break into termites' nests. With its long tongue, it sweeps up hundreds of insects at a time.

Anteaters have good hearing but poor eyesight

Thick fur protects anteater against bites and stings

BREAK FOR FOOD ▶
With its snout buried in a hollow log, a giant anteater flicks its tongue in and out to lap up its food. This massive South American animal is one of the largest insect-eating mammals, measuring up to 6 ft 6 in (2 m) long, including its bushy tail. It is also one of the few insect-eaters that are active by day. Giant anteaters are good at self-defense. They normally gallop away from trouble, but if they are cornered they rear up on the back legs and slash out with their front claws.

Long tongue can flick in and out 150 times a minute

◀ DESMAN SWIMMING
Most insect-eaters live on land. This Russian desman is one of the exceptions, because it dives for its prey in ponds and streams. Desmans are insectivores and are close relatives of moles, but they have webbed feet and flattened tails that work like a rudder. Most species live on aquatic insects, worms, and snails, but the Russian desman also eats frogs and fish. Desmans live in waterside burrows, and come out to feed at night.

Front claws are kept sharp because an anteater walks on its knuckles

CARNIVORES

A carnivore is any animal that eats meat. In the mammal world, there is a wide variety of hunters, such as marsupials, seals, and whales, but one group—known as the Carnivore order—contains about 250 species of the best-known hunters of all. It includes weasels, cats, dogs, and foxes, as well as bears, which are the largest predators on land. These carnivores hunt in different ways. Some stalk their prey on their own, while others work in teams. But all of them have specialized cheek teeth that work like scissors, slicing through flesh and cracking open bones.

▲ CARNIVORE SENSES
With its acute hearing, sensitive nose, and large eyes, the African palm civet is well-equipped for finding smaller animals after dark. It spends most of its time high up in trees, where it hunts other mammals and roosting birds. Like many carnivores, civets hunt by stealth, and they need keen senses to creep up on their prey. Once they are close enough, they launch a surprise attack.

Dappled skin gives leopard camouflage among the trees

◄ STORING FOOD
After killing an impala, this leopard has dragged the carcass into a tree. It is an impressive feat of strength, and also a good way of keeping scavengers at bay. Once the antelope is firmly wedged, the leopard will return to feed on it over several days. Many smaller carnivores, such as foxes, store food by burying it. This behavior, known as caching, gives them something to eat when prey is hard to find.

◄ UNDERWATER KILLER
Caught by a leopard seal, an Adélie penguin has little chance of escaping. The leopard seal is a fearsome hunter, with stabbing canine teeth. It uses these to grab penguins, and even other seals, before swallowing their flesh in chunks. Seals are closely related to land-based carnivores. Many scientists classify them in the Carnivore order, although their shape and lifestyle make them very distinct from mammals that hunt on land.

Seal's pointed canine teeth stab and grip the seal's prey

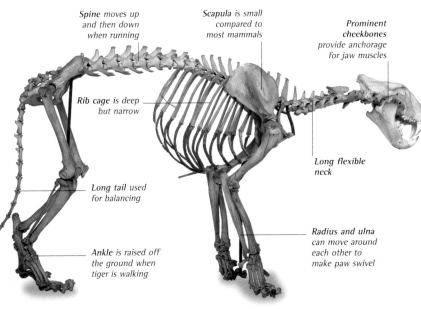

Spine *moves up and then down when running*

Scapula *is small compared to most mammals*

Prominent cheekbones *provide anchorage for jaw muscles*

Rib cage *is deep but narrow*

Long flexible neck

Long tail *used for balancing*

Ankle *is raised off the ground when tiger is walking*

Radius and ulna *can move around each other to make paw swivel*

▲ INSIDE A TIGER

Most carnivores—aside from bears—have skeletons that are built for flexibility and speed. In this skeleton, belonging to a tiger, a supple spine combines with long legs to give an extralarge stride. A tiger's front legs can swivel below the "elbow." This swiveling action is important when changing direction at speed, for example, when chasing prey. Bears walk on the soles of the feet, but many carnivores—including tigers—walk on the tips of their toes.

JAWS AND TEETH

Temporalis muscle

Upper carnassial tooth

Upper canine

Masseter muscle

Lower carnassial tooth

Lower canine

Most carnivores can open their mouths wide to deliver a fatal bite. The canine teeth, at the front of the jaw, stab into their victim, gripping it or killing it outright. Once the prey is dead, the carnassial teeth set to work. The upper and lower carnassials slide past each other when the jaw closes, slicing meat into manageable pieces. The power behind a carnivore's bite comes from two pairs of muscles, called the temporalis and masseter, which are attached to the jaw.

 carnivores

HUNTING TECHNIQUES

SOLITARY STALKER
Tigers hunt alone, using stealth and camouflage to catch their prey unawares. Despite their size—large tigers can weigh 660 lb (300 kg)—these exceptionally powerful predators attack from close quarters, instead of running down their prey in a chase. A tiger can spring over 33 ft (10 m) to make a kill, often knocking its prey over with the force of the impact.

PRECISION POUNCE
With all four feet in the air, this fox cub is pouncing on a rodent hidden in the grass. This hunting method is used by foxes and small cats in open habitats and sometimes in snow. Before pouncing, the hunter listens carefully for signs of movement, pinpointing the exact position of its prey. Foxes catch a variety of prey including birds, small mammals, and worms.

HUNTING BY WATER
Big cats usually avoid water, but the jaguar is an exception. It prefers to live near water and often hunts in water and marshy ground, catching rodents such as the capybara, as well as snakes, monkeys, deer, caimans, and fish. Jaguars also eat river turtles, puncturing the shells with their sharp canine teeth, before cracking them open with their jaws.

◀ HUNTING IN A GROUP

At the end of a successful chase, these African wild dogs have surrounded a wildebeest and are about to drag it to the ground. By hunting together, they can catch animals many times their size. African wild dogs are tireless runners, and they chase their prey at speeds up to 30 mph (50 km/h) until it tires and begins to slow down. Wolves hunt in a similar way, but groups of lions creep up on their victims before launching a surprise attack.

African wild dogs have distinctive coats—no two are alike

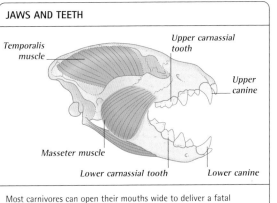

AVOIDING ATTACK

The natural world is a dangerous place. Predators are everywhere, and they can strike at any time. At the first sign of trouble, many mammals rely on speed to make their escape. Others freeze, and rely on their camouflage to escape from being seen. But some mammals react quite differently. Instead of running or hiding, they protect themselves with special defense systems, such as armor, spines, or evil-smelling fluids. These defenses are not foolproof, because predators are also well armed, but they give mammals a good chance of survival.

protection

Quills are hollow with sharp tips

▲ ARMOR PLATING
The three-banded armadillo has a hard shell that covers its back and the upper surface of its head and tail. When threatened, it curls up in a ball, with its soft underside hidden away, only unrolling when the danger has passed. This works well for adult armadillos, whose shells are thick and hard. But young armadillos are more vulnerable because their shells are softer.

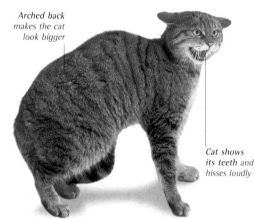

Arched back makes the cat look bigger

Cat shows its teeth and hisses loudly

▲ LOOKING DANGEROUS
If a wild cat is cornered by a predator, it reacts by making itself look as large and dangerous as possible. It stands side-on toward the aggressor, with its teeth bared and its back arched, and it hisses loudly whenever its enemy moves. The message is unmistakable: if it is attacked, it will fight back as viciously as it can. Domestic cats use the same defense system—it can stop dogs in their tracks.

COAT OF QUILLS ►
With its battery of sharp-tipped quills, this Cape porcupine can fend off the most determined predators, including leopards and lions. If it is in danger, it raises its quills and then rattles them together, warning its enemy not to approach. If that fails, the porcupine attacks: it turns its back on its attacker and suddenly reverses, stabbing its quills into its enemy's skin. The quills detach easily, leaving the predator with multiple injuries.

▲ COMPLETE CAMOUFLAGE
With its striped brown coat, this female greater kudu blends in beautifully with the dry scrubland around it. Greater kudus are some of Africa's biggest antelopes, but their secretive habits and camouflage make them difficult to see. Like many antelopes, females give birth in dense cover, and calves stay hidden while their mothers go off to feed. Antelope calves curl up and keep perfectly still if a predator is nearby.

▲ LEAP FOR FREEDOM
When chased by lions, impalas seem to burst into the air, taking leaps up to 10 ft (3 m) high and 35 ft (10 m) long. This explosion of movement often confuses the lions and helps the impalas to get away. Some grassland antelopes—such as gazelles—seem to attract attention when they are in danger, because they bounce high into the air with their legs held stiff and straight. This behavior is called stotting. It acts as a warning signal to the herd to flee the danger.

▲ CHEMICAL WEAPONS
Striped skunks give predators plenty of visual clues to warn against attack. If threatened, this skunk will stand on its front legs as a final warning. If the warning is ignored, the skunk ejects a foul-smelling liquid from glands underneath its tail, aiming it toward its enemy's face and eyes. The liquid causes intense irritation to the skin, and, at close range, can cause temporary blindness. The smell lingers for many days, and is so strong that humans can detect it up to 3,500 ft (1 km) downwind. There are ten species of skunk, and all of them have bold black-and-white markings to warn other animals not to come too close.

◀ KEEPING WATCH
For herd animals—like these wildebeest—staying alert is the key to survival. Like other grazing mammals, wildebeest cannot run away every time they see a predator. Instead, they keep the cheetah under observation, looking for any sign that it is about to attack. Cheetahs are short-distance sprinters, tiring quickly once they start to run. Wildebeest know this, and they keep the cheetah at a safe distance, giving themselves vital seconds if they need to escape. Cheetahs therefore rely on surprise to catch their prey off guard.

Migrating salmon provide bears with a protein-rich feast

OMNIVORES AND OPPORTUNISTS

Plant-eating monkeys may eat insects, and meat-eating wolves sometimes nibble plants. But for omnivores, eating varied foods is part of daily life. In the mammal world, omnivores include bears, pigs, raccoons, and foxes, as well as most humans. Omnivores change their menu with the seasons, eating whatever is available at different times of year. Opportunists also have varied diets, and are always on the lookout for a meal. In cities and towns, where food scraps get thrown away, this way of life is often a recipe for success.

Bear uses teeth to strip off berries

▲ FISHING TRIPS

Chest-deep in icy water, this Alaskan brown bear is catching salmon as they migrate inland to breed. In Alaska, salmon fishing is an important part of the bears' year. In early summer, dozens of bears gather together in rocky rapids, grabbing the fish as they leap upstream. Brown bears are strong enough to kill a horse, but despite their size, meat makes up less than one-quarter of their food. In the fall, bears can eat continuously without feeling full. They eat thousands of berries to increase their weight for their winter sleep.

▼ LOOKING FOR SCRAPS

Standing up on its back legs, a red fox peers into a garbage can. In some parts of the world—such as Britain—red foxes have adapted to city life. They patrol the streets between dusk and dawn, checking for food that has been thrown away. In North America, the raccoon behaves in a very similar way. Unlike the red fox, it is a very nimble climber, and it often sorts through garbage with its paws.

Lid was flipped off by fox's snout

HUMANS AS OMNIVORES

The earliest humans lived by hunting, and by gathering plant food from the wild. To do this successfully, they had to keep on the move, going to new places when trees were in fruit, or berries ripe and ready for collection. But about 10,000 years ago, people started to raise animals, and to cultivate plants for food. This was the beginning of farming—a new way of life that has changed the face of the world. Today, about 35 percent of the Earth's surface is used for farming, and in some regions, room for new farmland is hard to find. These narrow terraces, on a steep hillside in Indonesia, are used for growing rice.

STRANGE ALLIANCES ▼

Many mammals—from bears to humans—enjoy the taste of honey. In Africa, the ratel or honey badger has a remarkable way of tracking down this food. It follows a bird called the honeyguide, which flits from branch to branch, leading the way toward wild bees' nests. Once the ratel is at a nest, it breaks it open with its claws. The ratel feeds on the honey and bee grubs, while the honeyguide gets the beeswax as its share of the bounty.

Thick fur protects the ratel from bee stings

Ratel's strong jaws can kill animals several times its size

▲ FEEDING FRENZY

Rats are supreme opportunists. Intelligent and agile, they scuttle through burrows and buildings, and they have a keen sense of smell, which helps them to find food. The ones shown here are black rats—a species notorious for spreading disease. Black rats often live indoors, and live mainly on plant food. Brown rats are bigger and have a more varied diet. They are adaptable animals and live in all kinds of habitats, including cities.

CLEANING UP LEFTOVERS ▼

Watched by a pair of jackals, these two spotted hyenas are feeding on the remains of an antelope. Part-hunter, part-scavenger, hyenas have immensely powerful jaws, enabling them to rip through hides and crack open bones. Compared to hyenas, jackals are smaller and more timid. They often gather at hyena kills and steal anything they can get. In rural Africa, jackals and hyenas wander into settlements at night and scavenge anything edible that has been thrown away.

Spots on coat become fewer as hyena ages

omnivores

Front legs are longer than back ones

COURTSHIP AND MATING

Like all animals, mammals are driven by the urge to mate. Different species attract partners by using special calls, scents, and visual signs. Some species use elaborate courtship rituals to overcome their natural wariness of one another. Breeding patterns vary. In temperate and cold climates, most females come into breeding condition, called estrus, at a certain time of year, timed so that the young will be born when food is plentiful. Where conditions remain constant, mammals may breed at any time of year.

Bright colors on face show male is healthy and so more likely to attract a mate

▲ DEFEATING RIVALS

Male mammals often compete with one another to mate with the females. Some species use visual displays to put off rivals, but others have physical fights. Male giraffes have necking contests to establish which animal is strongest. The rivals stand side by side and take turns swinging their heads at one another's necks.

◄ ATTRACTING A PARTNER

Visual signals and body language are effective ways of attracting a mate at close quarters. In many species of mammal, the males are larger and more conspicuous. Male mandrills are more than twice the size of the females, with brightly colored faces and bottoms. Research shows that the males with the brightest colors are the ones most likely to mate. A dominant male leads a mixed group of about 20 mandrills and fathers all the young.

Strutting gait and aggressive stance warn rival males away

▲ LASTING BOND

Small antelopes called dik-dik, such as these, are among the few species in which males and females form a lasting pair bond. Most mammals establish only fleeting bonds with their partners. Rodents and many other species are promiscuous—they mate with many partners, then go their separate ways.

Flippers used to maintain position in water

▲ COURTSHIP SONG

Sounds travel a long way under water. Marine mammals, such as whales, sing complex songs to locate a mate in the vast spaces of the oceans. Humpback whales like this are renowned for their beautiful songs in which many different sounds are strung together, including squeals, sighs, and roars. During the breeding season, which falls in winter, humpbacks make long journeys all the way from polar seas to the tropics to breed.

MATING: DURATION

BRIEF ENCOUNTER

In mammals, fertilization takes place inside the female's body, where the male's sperm unites with the female's egg. The fertilized egg then develops into a young mammal. The time taken in mating varies, lasting only a few seconds in species such as hyraxes, above, and also whales.

PROLONGED MATING

Rhinos are generally solitary, with each animal keeping to its own patch. Male rhinos are strongly territorial and will drive off other males. During the breeding season, a male herds any females he comes across into his territory. Mating lasts for several hours.

Female's body language shows she is willing to mate

◄ KING FOR A SEASON

Lionesses live in groups, called prides, which cooperate in hunting. The group also contains one or two males that spend most of their time patrolling and driving off rival males. The dominant male's control of the pride rarely lasts longer than two or three years, after which he is ousted by a stronger rival. When a challenger takes over, he kills all the young cubs fathered by his predecessor, so that the lionesses come into estrus again, since they are no longer suckling young.

Nose can smell when female is in estrus

mating

PLACENTAL MAMMALS

Mammals are divided into three groups according to the way their young develop. The largest group by far is the placental mammals or eutheria, whose young develop to an advanced stage in their mother's uterus, or womb. Here the unborn baby is nourished by a temporary organ called the placenta. The mother provides her fetus (unborn young) with nourishment and oxygen. The period during which the baby develops before birth is called gestation. Gestation times vary greatly between different mammals.

Baby gorilla is born at an advanced stage of development

Umbilical cord links unborn baby to the placenta

Placenta is a temporary, blood-rich organ embedded in the wall of the womb

Mother's abdomen swells as baby grows

◀ DEVELOPING IN THE UTERUS
This model shows an unborn baby gorilla developing in the mother's uterus. After mating, the fertilized egg embeds in the wall of the uterus and divides many times to become a fetus. The baby's blood passes down the umbilical cord into the tissue of the placenta, where it runs alongside the mother's blood. Nutrients and oxygen pass from the mother to the baby, while carbon dioxide and waste pass the opposite way. The baby gorilla is born after about nine months.

THE MOMENT OF BIRTH

ENCOURAGING THE CALF TO ITS FEET

STANDING FOR THE FIRST TIME

▲ GIVING BIRTH
African elephants have the longest gestation of any mammal, up to 22 months. When the baby is fully developed, powerful muscles in the mother's womb begin to tighten rhythmically, to squeeze it down the birth canal. The newly born calf lies on the ground, still surrounded by the fetal membrane, which is pale in color.

▲ A GENTLE NUDGE
The female elephant (called a cow) gives birth within the safety of a herd, made up of other females and their young. Soon after birth, the placenta also comes away from the uterus and is expelled. Other experienced females gather around and may help by removing the protective fetal membrane that surrounded the baby in the womb. They may also assist the mother in gently nudging the calf to its feet.

▲ WELL-DEVELOPED BABY
A newborn African elephant calf weighs 265 lbs (120 kg). Only minutes after birth, it is able to stand and starts to suckle milk from the teats between its mother's fore legs. The baby will stay close to its mother, suckling milk until it is about two years old and its tusks start to grow. It will be dependent on its mother for about 10 years.

LITTER SIZES

HORSE (1)
Litter sizes (the number of young born at one time) vary greatly among placental mammals. In general, the larger species tend to have long gestation periods and give birth to only a few young. Most horses give birth to one foal after eleven and a half months.

HAMSTER (6–8)
Small mammals, such as rodents, generally have much shorter gestation times and give birth to larger litters than large mammals. Hamsters have one of the shortest gestation times, giving birth after only 15–16 days. Most hamster litters contain between six and eight young.

DOG (3–8)
Dogs, like this labrador bitch, give birth to a litter of 3–10 puppies some 63 days after mating. Domestic dogs are descended from wolves, which produce similar-sized litters after the same length gestation. African hunting dogs have the largest litters of any canid, up to 16 pups.

HUMAN (1–4)
After a pregnancy lasting 267 days on average, human mothers give birth to usually just one child, more rarely twins, triplets, or even quadruplets. Humans spend more time raising their young than any other mammal, and human babies take the longest time to grow up.

HELPLESS YOUNG ►
The young of all placental mammals are born at an advanced stage compared to pouched mammals and monotremes. However, some are much more fully formed than others. Newborn baby mice, rats, and these rabbits lack fur and are helpless. Unable to see, hear, or stand, the babies are totally dependent on the mother, who keeps them warm while they suckle her milk. Young rabbits grow quickly and can breed at three months old.

◄ INDEPENDENT YOUNG
Large hoofed mammals, like these wildebeest, are born after a much longer gestation of eight and a half months. The newborn calf has reached a more advanced stage of development, with eyes and ears open and a protective coat of hair. In the open African grasslands, the baby is at great risk from predators, but is able to struggle to its feet in just 3–5 minutes. After half an hour, it can keep up with the herd and so travel in relative safety.

Newborn dolphin calf is well-developed and able to swim immediately

Baby dolphin emerges tail-first

▲ BIRTH IN MARINE MAMMALS
Among marine mammals, seals bear their young on land or ice, but whales, dolphins, manatees, and dugongs give birth in water. Female dolphins, like this one, produce their young in the upper waters, so the baby can surface quickly to breathe. As with elephants, the mother gives birth within a group of females that provide safety and often assistance. The mother or another female dives below the newborn calf's body and guides it to the surface for its first breath of air.

placental mammals

POUCHED MAMMALS

Pouched mammals (called metatheria or marsupials) are the second-largest group of mammals. After developing in the mother's uterus for just a few weeks, the tiny young are born before they are fully formed. They must latch on to the mother's teat to obtain nourishment. The teats are usually located in a pouch on her stomach, but a few types, like the mouse opossum, have no true pouch. Most pouched mammals live in Australasia, but some opossums dwell in Central and South America, and the Virginia opossum lives in North America.

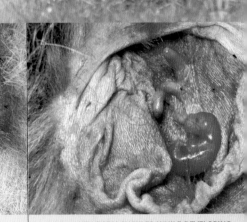

RED KANGAROO AND JOEY ▶
Pouched mammals of Australasia vary greatly in size, shape, and habits. The group includes plant-eaters such as kangaroos, wombats, and koalas, meat-eating predators such as Tasmanian devils; and also omnivores. The red kangaroo is the world's largest pouched mammal. The baby, called a joey, is carried in a pouch that holds it securely as the mother hops around feeding, or even bounds along at great speed. This form of locomotion is very energy efficient.

Joey's head peeks out of pouch

Long leg bones hold pouch and baby well above the ground

FEMALE REPRODUCTIVE SYSTEM

uterus

ovary

ovary

uterus

lateral vagina

lateral vagina

birth canal

ovary

ovary

uterus

vagina

POUCHED MAMMAL

PLACENTAL MAMMAL

The reproductive parts of female pouched and placental mammals are very different. While the young of placental mammals develop within the single uterus and eventually pass down the vagina, pouched mammals have two uteri and two vaginas, with a separate birth canal. A fertilized egg spends only a few weeks developing in the uterus before passing down the birth canal and out of the mother. In some pouched mammals, the birth canal develops for every birth.

pouched mammals

NEWBORN WALLABY BEGINS JOURNEY TO POUCH

▲ CRAWLING TO THE SAFETY OF THE POUCH
Like all pouched mammals, baby kangaroos and wallabies like this tammar wallaby are born in an embryonic state. Blind and naked, the baby looks completely helpless, but its front legs are relatively well-developed. It uses these to begin an epic journey from the birth opening to the safety of its mother's pouch.

NEWBORN WALLABY ENTERS POUCH

▲ ENTERING THE POUCH
With eyes and ears closed, the tiny baby seeks the shelter of the pouch by instinct and by using its sense of touch and smell. The mother can only help by licking a path through her fur for the joey to follow. This amazing journey is very tiring for the baby, but lasts only a few minutes. Once in the pouch, the baby wallaby clamps on to one of its mother's four teats and begins to suck.

NEWBORN SUCKLES WHILE DEVELOPING

▲ ATTACHED TO NIPPLE INSIDE POUCH
Once the baby clamps onto the nipple, the nipple swells so the tiny mammal cannot let go until it is fully formed. This ensures that it does not let go of the nipple as its mother hops around. Fed by the mother's rich milk, the baby grows quickly. Its eyes and ears open, fur grows on its body, and the long, strong hind legs develop.

▲ FAST BREEDER

Bandicoots are long-nosed pouched mammals from Australia and New Guinea. They are mostly insect-eaters. This eastern barred bandicoot is one of the quickest breeders in the mammal kingdom. Four to five babies are born after 11 days' gestation and then spend around 60 days in the pouch. The young themselves are able to breed at just three months.

Young cling to mother's fur with well-developed claws

▲ MEAT-EATING PREDATOR

At up to 32 in (80 cm) long, Tasmanian devils are the largest carnivorous pouched mammals. They hunt prey ranging in size from insects to possums, wallabies, and even sheep, and also eat carrion (dead animals). A litter of up to four young are born after 30-31 days. These spend the next 15 weeks in the mother's pouch, and move on to solid food at about 20 weeks.

◄ POUCHLESS MOUSE OPOSSUM

South American opossums are a family of mostly rat-sized, tree-dwelling mammals. Their long, scaly tails wrap around branches as they clamber around. Almost all metatheria carry their young in a pouch, but some opossums have no pouch, while others carry their young in two flaps of skin on their bellies. Offspring are firmly attached to nipples on their mother's belly at first, but as they grow older, they are carried on her back. South American opossums produce up to ten young after two and a half week's gestation.

◄ WELL-GROWN JOEY

After a few months, the joey begins to peek out of the pouch. At around six months, its mother gives it a first proper taste of the outside world by gently tipping it onto the ground. Thereafter it spends more and more time out of the pouch, hopping back in at the first sign of danger. It continues to suckle throughout its first year. At 18 months, it can produce young of its own.

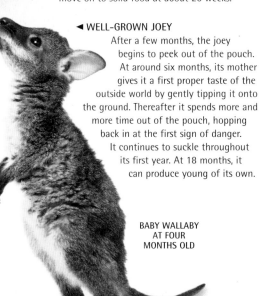

BABY WALLABY
AT FOUR
MONTHS OLD

Tiny eyes are hidden by the soft, cream-colored fur

▼ MARSUPIAL MOLE

Marsupial moles dwell in the sandy deserts and scrublands of Australia. They "swim" through the loose sand using their powerful front claws to shovel the grains aside. A burrowing lifestyle has led this species to evolve a similar body shape to other moles—placental mammals to which it is only very distantly related. Females bear 1-2 young that are carried in a pouch that faces backward, so it does not fill with sand.

MONOTREMES

The small group of monotremes contains just five species—four species of echidna and the duck-billed platypus, all of which are found in Australia. Monotremes resemble reptiles in that they lay eggs, making them unique among mammals. Certain body systems are similar to reptiles. Their digestive, reproductive, and urinary systems empty from a single exit, giving the name monotreme (meaning one hole). But monotremes are mammals and produce milk to feed their young.

Hind feet are partly webbed to aid maneuvers

ODD COMBINATION ▶
The platypus looks like a cross between several different animals, with a ducklike bill, molelike body, broad, beaverlike tail, and webbed feet, like an otter. The first specimens to reach Europe in about 1800 were thought to be fakes made by combining parts of various animals. In fact, the platypus's unusual features help it to find food in water, with webbed feet acting as flippers, the tail as a rudder, and the bill as a sensing device.

Bill is soft and leathery, not hard like a duck's

Webbed, clawed front feet used for paddling

▲ POISONED SPUR
The male platypus has sharp spurs on the ankles of its hind feet. This hollow spike is linked to a gland containing poison strong enough to kill another platypus. Scientists believe that the animal uses its weapon to threaten rivals in the breeding season. Echidnas also have spurs, but do not inject poison.

◀ PLATYPUS WAY OF LIFE
Platypuses inhabit the banks of streams and pools in eastern Australia and neighboring Tasmania. They catch insect larvae, shrimps, and crayfish by diving underwater and feeling for victims with their sensitive bills. The bill can also pick up tiny electrical pulses given off by its preys' muscles. The platypus stores food in its cheek pouches while diving. Then it comes ashore to grind up its meal with horny ridges in its bill.

ECHIDNA EGG IN POUCH

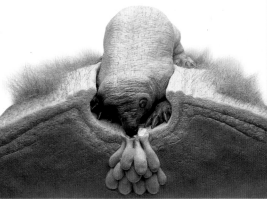

LAPPING FROM MILK PATCHES IN THE POUCH

SNUG NESTS

▲ LEATHERY-SHELLED EGG
Both female echidnas and platypuses lay eggs, but they are kept in different ways. During the breeding season, the short-nosed echidna develops a pouch on her belly. Three weeks after mating, she lays an egg and transfers it to her pouch and incubates it with her body heat. The platypus lays one to three eggs in a burrow and warms her eggs by curling around them.

▲ RICH MILK
After 10 days of incubation, the young echidna hatches out from its leathery egg. The mother's milk is not supplied by teats as in other mammals. Instead, the undeveloped baby laps milk from special patches in its mother's pouch. Baby platypuses also hatch about 10 days after laying. These tiny young lap nutritious milk that oozes from nipplelike patches on their mother's abdomen.

▲ GROWING UP
The baby echidna lives in the mother's pouch for the first 55 days of its life. Then the mother leaves it in her burrow when she goes out to look for food. This continues for seven months. Young platypuses remain in the burrow for three to four months. The mother seals the entrance when she goes out. After this time, the young must fend for themselves.

FINDING FOOD ▶
Various species of echidna have different diets. Short-nosed species feed mainly on ants and termites—hence their common name, spiny anteaters. They tear open the insects' nests with their stout claws and slurp them up with their sticky tongues. Long-nosed echidnas, shown here, mainly eat earthworms. Lacking teeth, echidnas mash their prey using sharp spines in their mouths. Echidnas may hunt by day or night.

Long, sharp spines are modified hairs

Large, clawed feet aid digging

Beak curves upward

Ball of prickly spines deters most predators

▲ UNUSUAL ECHIDNAS
The echidna is just as extraordinary-looking as the platypus, with a long, beaklike snout, spiny body, and large, clawed front feet. Short-nosed echidnas like this one are far more common than their long-nosed cousins, being found throughout Australia and also in New Guinea. Long-nosed echidnas, found only in the highlands of New Guinea, are larger but less spiny. Recently, two new species of long-nosed echidna have been identified.

monotremes

DEFENSE IN SPINY ECHIDNAS ▲
Echidnas have several defenses against predators such as foxes and dingoes. When threatened, they may roll up into a tight ball, which enemies find difficult to penetrate, or they may quickly burrow underground, leaving only the tops of their spines showing. Spines cover their entire bodies, including their tails and ear openings. Echidnas also burrow underground to escape extreme heat in summer and cold in the highlands in winter. During this time their body temperature drops to save energy.

EARLY LIFE

Mammals use huge amounts of energy rearing their young compared to most other animals. A mammal's first food is the mother's milk, which contains all the nourishment the youngster needs as well as antibodies to ward off disease. In mammals such as hares and mice, the nursing period, during which the babies drink milk, lasts only a week or two. In elephants, rhinos, and other large mammals, nursing lasts for several years. In the vast majority of mammals, the female alone cares for the young, but in a few species, such as marmosets, fathers also help.

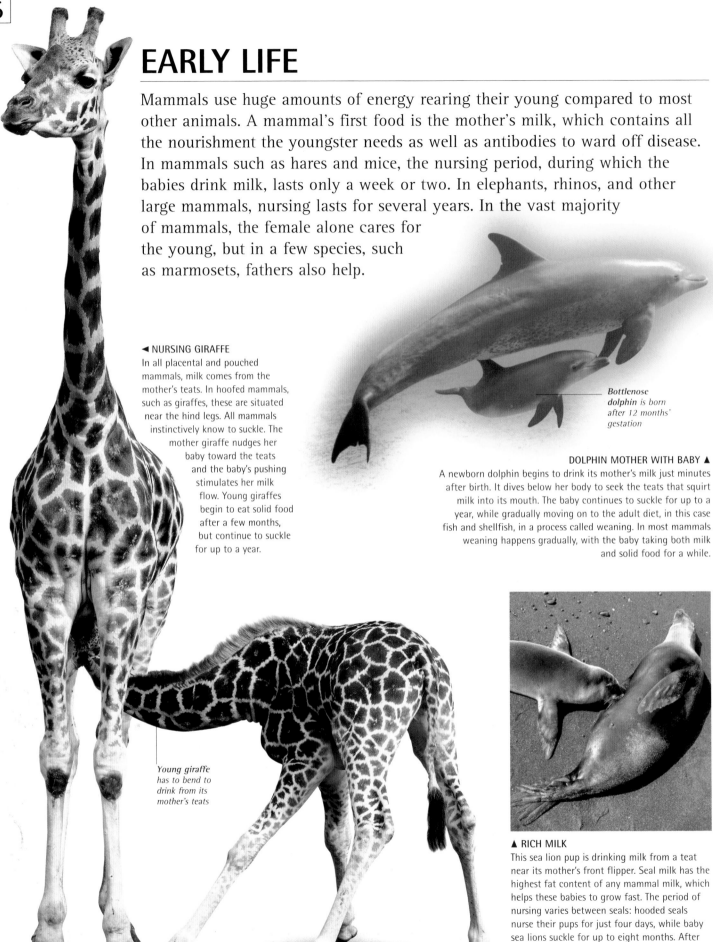

◄ NURSING GIRAFFE
In all placental and pouched mammals, milk comes from the mother's teats. In hoofed mammals, such as giraffes, these are situated near the hind legs. All mammals instinctively know to suckle. The mother giraffe nudges her baby toward the teats and the baby's pushing stimulates her milk flow. Young giraffes begin to eat solid food after a few months, but continue to suckle for up to a year.

Bottlenose dolphin is born after 12 months' gestation

DOLPHIN MOTHER WITH BABY ▲
A newborn dolphin begins to drink its mother's milk just minutes after birth. It dives below her body to seek the teats that squirt milk into its mouth. The baby continues to suckle for up to a year, while gradually moving on to the adult diet, in this case fish and shellfish, in a process called weaning. In most mammals weaning happens gradually, with the baby taking both milk and solid food for a while.

Young giraffe has to bend to drink from its mother's teats

▲ RICH MILK
This sea lion pup is drinking milk from a teat near its mother's front flipper. Seal milk has the highest fat content of any mammal milk, which helps these babies to grow fast. The period of nursing varies between seals: hooded seals nurse their pups for just four days, while baby sea lions suckle for up to eight months. After just eight days ashore with her baby, the mother goes back to sea for a few days at a time, returning regularly to nurse her pup.

FAST GROWERS

BIRTH DAY
Some mammal babies take many years to grow up, but house mice mature amazingly quickly. The female gives birth to a litter of up to 10 young just 20 days after mating. The helpless babies are born in a nest of straw, grass, and moss, which helps to keep them warm.

TWO DAYS OLD
Newborn mice are blind, hairless, and hardly recognizable as rodents. They are completely dependent on the mother, who suckles them and curls her body around them to keep them warm. However, eyes, limbs, and tails start to develop just two days after birth.

FOUR DAYS OLD
At four days old, the young are starting to look a little more like adult mice, with ears, limbs, and other features continuing to develop. They squeak to attract the mother's attention if they feel cold or hungry, and have begun to squirm and wriggle around in the nest.

SIX DAYS OLD
At six days old, the babies' fur has grown. They still spend much time asleep or suckling, but are becoming increasingly active. At this age, their louder squeaks may attract predators, but the mother will breed again and quickly produce another litter if this one is lost.

FOURTEEN DAYS OLD
At two weeks old, the young mice have begun to spend time out of the nest, exploring their environment. They now begin to eat seeds and grain, and will soon be weaned off their mother's milk. In another few days they will leave the nest for good and fend for themselves.

INTENSIVE CARE ▶
Most primate mothers carry their youngsters with them as they move around the trees in search of food. The young may either ride on the mother's back or cling to her belly, like this baby mona monkey. Apes and monkeys give birth to far fewer young than rodents, but spend much longer looking after their offspring. This mona monkey baby will spend a year with its mother before having to fend for itself.

young

Hands have opposable thumbs to keep a firm hold on branches

Baby suckles when the mother stops to feed

◀ CARING FATHERS
In most mammals, care of the young is left entirely to the female. Wolves, however, have a litter of between four and seven cubs, which are cared for by both parents. Living in a pack, even other adults help to look after the young. Each pack has a strict hierarchy in which only the most senior male and female, called the alpha pair, are allowed to breed and produce offspring. By helping the seniors, junior animals gain experience in rearing young, which will come in handy if they leave to start a pack of their own.

Tail helps to balance the extra weight of the baby

GROWING AND LEARNING

Many mammals continue to care for their young long after the babies have finished suckling. While small species, such as rodents, quickly become independent, young primates, whales, and female elephants remain in the same group for life. By copying the behavior of their parent and sometimes other adults, young mammals learn survival skills such as how to find food and avoid danger. Babies growing up in mammal groups learn how to relate to other group members. All species of mammal also learn through play.

growing

Orangutan's feet and hands have excellent grip and flexibility

◄ A LOT TO LEARN
Young primates spend more time growing up than other mammals. A female will probably only raise three or four young during her 20 years of fertile adulthood. This baby orangutan will stay with its mother for a total of about eight years. In addition to acquiring physical skills and coordination, the baby finds out about the world around it through trial and error. Young primates are naturally curious and will pick up and investigate any unfamiliar object they find.

◄ FED BY THE PACK
Group bonds are unusually strong among canids (members of the dog family). African hunting dogs live in a pack in which all adults help to provide food for the young. After suckling their mother's milk for three months, the babies move on to solid food brought back by the hunters. When the pup whines and licks the adult's face to show it is hungry, the hunter regurgitates (coughs up) a meal of half-chewed meat.

◄ HUNTING SKILLS
European otters give birth to up to three cubs in riverbank burrows. Blind and helpless at birth, the babies learn to swim by two months old. At three months, they move on to solid food, but may stay with their mother for up to a year. The female demonstrates how to catch fish and releases half-dead prey so her offspring can practice their hunting skills. Young otters are playful, chasing one another and slithering down muddy banks.

Playful nips help fox cubs learn how to use their teeth

EARLY INDEPENDENCE ▶
In small mammals such as rodents, the young become independent soon after they finish suckling. At just a few months old, a young gray squirrel leaves the nest to fend for itself. With little chance to learn from its mother, survival techniques, such as hoarding nuts in the fall and shinning up trees to escape danger, come partly by instinct. This young animal will soon reach maturity and start to produce litters of its own.

▲ PLAYTIME
Young mammals like these fox cubs spend a lot of time playing with brothers and sisters. In all mammals, mock fights help to strengthen growing limbs, while young hunters learn stalking and pouncing skills. Play fighting helps young foxes learn their place within the family group. The cubs also spend time exploring, which teaches them more about the environment in which they live.

▲ LEAVING HOME
In the grasslands of Africa, cheetahs produce a litter of two to four young. Like other young carnivores, the cubs spend a lot of time wrestling as they learn to use sharp teeth and claws. The running skills of the adults develop as the cubs chase after one another and even use their tolerant parent as target practice. After 13-20 months, it is time to leave the mother, but siblings, especially brothers, may remain together for years.

ELEPHANT UP TO 77 YEARS

DOLPHIN UP TO 65 YEARS

HIPPO UP TO 54 YEARS

CHIMP UP TO 53 YEARS

RHINO UP TO 50 YEARS

BISON UP TO 40 YEARS

POLAR BEAR UP TO 38 YEARS

TIGER UP TO 26 YEARS

RABBIT UP TO 10 YEARS

MOUSE UP TO 6 YEARS

◀ GROWING OLD
In general, larger mammals live longer than smaller ones, with whales, elephants, and hippos being among the longest-lived species. With the help of modern medicine, humans live the longest of all. Small species, such as rodents, seldom live more than a year in the wild, but survive longer in captivity. Mammals without natural enemies are more likely to live longer than prey creatures, who rarely evade their predators for very long.

▼ ELEPHANT HERDS
Elephant calves spend several years growing up in the safe world of the herd, made up of several females and their young. The babies learn physical skills such as how to use their trunks by watching the adults, and also how group life works. Adult males are only allowed to join the herd for mating, and so the young males are driven out when they reach maturity. Females stay and continue the learning process as they help to raise younger calves.

INTELLIGENCE

Mammals have large brains and are generally intelligent, but how is intelligence defined? Many scientists define it as the ability to learn—to use information stored in the memory to make decisions, and solve problems. Apes, dolphins, and rodents can solve problems to a lesser or greater extent. Intelligence is related to adaptability (the ability to change behavior to suit changing conditions) which allows mammals, such as monkeys, to do well in new environments. It is also linked to communication.

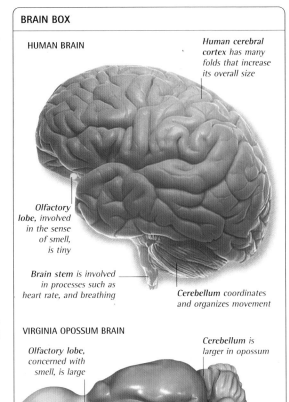

BRAIN BOX

HUMAN BRAIN

Human cerebral cortex has many folds that increase its overall size

Olfactory lobe, involved in the sense of smell, is tiny

Brain stem is involved in processes such as heart rate, and breathing

Cerebellum coordinates and organizes movement

VIRGINIA OPOSSUM BRAIN

Olfactory lobe, concerned with smell, is large

Cerebellum is larger in opossum

Cerebral cortex, involved in learning, is relatively small

Brain stem

The cerebral cortex, shown in pink above, is the "thinking" part of the brain that stores and processes information. In mammals such as primates, this part of the brain is large and well-developed compared to species such as the Virginia opossum. In humans, the cerebral cortex is deeply folded, which increases its surface area.

In the opossum, the olfactory lobe, here colored yellow, used for smell, is well-developed, reflecting the animal's reliance on this sense. The size of a mammal's brain in relation to its body size is sometimes seen as a measure of intelligence. In elephants the brain to body ratio is 1:650; in dolphins it is 1:125; and in humans it is 1:40. This makes humans seem more intelligent than elephants or dolphins.

Flat stone chosen to provide surface for cracking shells

◄ SEA OTTER USING TOOLS
The ability to use tools is often seen as a mark of intelligence. Sea otters smash hard-shelled clams and sea urchins on a flat stone held on their chest to get at the soft flesh inside. They have been observed making repeated dives to find a suitable stone. Birds such as thrushes use stones in a similar way, dashing snails against rocks to break their shells. Sea otters also use seaweed to anchor themselves while sleeping at night. They wrap it around themselves to stop from drifting away.

◄ PRIMATE INTELLIGENCE
Chimpanzees are our closest relatives in the mammal world. They use a variety of tools, for example, poking sticks inside termite mounds to disturb the insects, which they then spoon into their mouths. Several birds, including the Galapagos finch, also use sticks in this way, but the chimp shapes its tool to make it more efficient, removing side shoots so the stick reaches farther, which suggests the ape has the ability to form a mental image of the tool at work. In research centers, chimps have been trained to use sign language—and even computer keyboards marked with special symbols to communicate with humans.

▲ COOPERATIVE HUNTING

Cetaceans are intelligent creatures. Several species of whale and dolphin are known to hunt in groups, either surrounding a shoal of fish or herding them into the shallows, as shown here. In research centers, dolphins have been trained to respond to a variety of human commands. Tests suggest that they can share learned information with each other using sounds. However, it is difficult to measure cetacean intelligence, as their environment is so different from ours.

▲ HUMAN INTELLIGENCE

Human use of tools, such as hand axes, dates back more than 2.5 million years. In addition, people have used complex spoken language and written symbols to communicate for thousands of years. We can build all sorts of structures and find new ways of growing food to feed the world's population. More recently, technology has allowed us to land on the Moon (above), investigate the ocean depths, and—through modern medicine—even extend the human life span.

USING CANID INTELLIGENCE

Wolves, foxes, and other wild canids are clever and adaptable, being able to exploit new food sources when the chance arises—for example, to raid henhouses and steal chickens. Domestic dogs are descended from wolves. Over many centuries, careful breeding has produced a variety of dogs that can be trained to help humans. Various breeds are used to herd sheep, guide blind people, track criminals, and detect survivors in destroyed buildings, as shown above.

intelligence

PROBLEM SOLVING ▲

Rodents are quick at some kinds of learning. Rats can learn to make their way through mazes. Squirrels are able to navigate complex obstacle courses to reach a food reward, not only crossing barriers such as tightropes, but also learning to operate a sequence of levers and knobs. This demonstrates memory. Adaptability has allowed rodents to colonize many new habitats, including towns and cities.

Arms longer than legs

PRIMATES

Primates are a diverse order of mainly forest-dwelling mammals. This group includes apes, monkeys, and also humans. Primates have grasping feet, hairy bodies, and rounded faces with forward-facing eyes that provide good vision. The classification of primates has recently been revised. The order is divided into two groups: the Strepsirhini or "primitive" primates, including lemurs, lorises, galagos, and pottos, and the Haplorhini, or higher primates, which include apes, monkeys, and tarsiers (a group of small, nocturnal primates).

Dense shaggy fur covers most of body

Arms used to swing from tree to tree, using body weight like a pendulum

▲ THE GROUP OF APES

Scientists divide apes into great and lesser apes. The great apes consist of gorillas, orangutans, chimpanzees, and humans. The group of lesser apes is made up of gibbons, such as this siamang. Apes have long muscular arms, which some use to swing through the trees. This form of movement is called brachiation. Siamangs are forest-dwellers that live in small family units.

Female macaque grooms her baby to get rid of grime and parasites

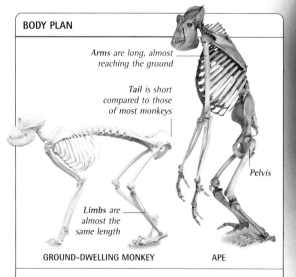

BODY PLAN

Arms are long, almost reaching the ground

Tail is short compared to those of most monkeys

Pelvis

Limbs are almost the same length

GROUND-DWELLING MONKEY   APE

The skeletons of monkeys and apes show certain differences. Monkeys' bodies are generally adapted to movement on all fours, with hind limbs a little longer than forelimbs. Monkeys that live in trees have long tails that they use for balance and sometimes gripping, though this macaque has a short tail. Apes, such as gorillas, have no tails, and a flatter face, broad chest, and mobile arms. The structure and angle of the pelvis allows it a more upright stance.

◄ CARE OF YOUNG

Most primates give birth to just one young at a time, more rarely twins. Mothers, like this macaque, devote years to rearing their offspring. For example, young chimpanzees and gorillas suckle their mother's milk for up to four years. Most primates live in groups, varying in size from small family units to troops of several hundred individuals. All groups involve a hierarchy, with senior animals dominating younger ones.

Leathery palms provide nonslip grip

Single swing can cover 10 ft (3 m)

primates

MOVEMENT

WALKING UPRIGHT
Great apes, like humans, chimps and this gorilla, are bipedal—able to stand upright and walk on their hind legs. Apes also climb well, and several make nests in trees at night. Apes such as orangutans swing from branch to branch using their long arms. Gorillas are powerfully muscled and are very strong.

ON ALL FOURS
Most primates are quadrupeds, moving on all fours. Their arms and legs are of roughly equal length. The baboons shown here live in open country, where they spend most of their time on the ground, running or walking on four limbs. They also climb well and scamper up trees or high rocks when danger threatens.

CLINGING AND LEAPING
Lemurs are a group of forest-dwelling primates from Madagascar. With the body held upright, they leap between branches and cling on using their strong limbs. Many species have a long tail. On the ground, the sifaka, shown here, bounds along sideways on its springy hind legs, using its arms for balance.

Elongated finger

Opposable big toe

Fingers with rounded pads

Grooming claws

Mobile fingers

Gap between big toe and other toes is large

AYE-AYE HAND

AYE-AYE FOOT

TARSIER HAND

TARSIER FOOT

CHIMPANZEE HAND

CHIMPANZEE FOOT

▲ HANDS AND FEET
Primates have five digits on each hand and foot. In most species, one large finger and toe can be opposed—set against the others, forming an effective grasp. Hands and feet are adapted to different lifestyles. Aye-ayes are a type of lemur with clawed hands and feet for gripping. One extralong finger is used to hook grubs out from under tree bark. Tarsiers have rounded pads on their feet and hands for climbing. Chimpanzees have mobile, nimble hands and feet.

▲ NEW WORLD MONKEYS
Monkeys are divided into two groups according to their distribution. New World monkeys are found in Central and South America, Old World monkeys in Africa and Asia. New World monkeys include marmosets, tamarins, and this spider monkey. They have broad noses with sideways-facing nostrils. With thumbs that are not opposable, these mostly forest-dwelling primates leap between trees with a squirrel-like movement. Spider monkeys have long limbs and a prehensile (gripping) tail.

Long nose may help male to attract mates

OLD WORLD MONKEYS ▶
Baboons, guenons, macaques, mandrills, langurs, colobus, and this proboscis monkey are all Old World species. Often larger than New World monkeys, they inhabit varied habitats including forests, swamps, and grasslands. Many are active during the day. They have hard pads on their rumps for sitting, and narrow noses with nostrils facing forward or downward. Proboscis monkeys live in small troops made up of one male and between six and 10 females and their young.

GROUP LIFE

Some types of mammals live alone and only come together to mate and raise their young. Other species are social—living in groups that range from small family units to herds hundreds of animals strong. Group life may allow mammals to find food and avoid danger more easily. Predators such as lions, wolves, and dolphins hunt in cooperative groups, while herds or troops of prey mammals have many pairs of eyes to watch for predators. In some groups, all the adults help to rear the young. One possible disadvantage is that group members have to share food, which can be difficult when food is scarce.

MEERKAT COLONY ►
In South Africa, meerkats live in colonies of 30-50 animals in a network of underground burrows. These mammals, members of the mongoose family, have well-organized societies, in which group members share the care of the young. While searching for food, adult meerkats take turns acting as sentries. When a lookout spots a predator such as a snake or hawk, it gives a warning bark and the whole group runs for cover.

group life

Forward-facing eyes provide good vision

Sentries scan for danger in different directions

Lioness holds wildebeest to prevent its escape

Lioness kills the victim by biting its throat while others hold it down

◄ HUNTING UNIT
Almost uniquely among cats, lions are social animals. Many prides consist of 6-12 members: mostly lionesses and their cubs, with one or two males that are often brothers. The lions defend their pride from other males, while the lionesses do most of the hunting and may even suckle one another's cubs. Working as a team allows the pride to tackle large prey such as zebra and buffalo, which would evade one lioness hunting on her own.

Young are cared
for by the colony

*Standing on
hind legs* helps
meerkats to
spot enemies

Elephant calves grow up within
the safety of the herd

▲ LED BY THE FEMALE

In the grasslands of Africa, female savannah elephants and their young
live in close-knit groups of about ten animals. The herd is led by the
most experienced female, called the matriarch, who guides her group
to grazing and water. When a calf is born, all the females will help to
rear and protect it. Baby elephants rarely stray more than a trunk's
length from their mother when small.

Male is distinguished by
his size and a ruff of
hair around the neck

▲ MALE IN CHARGE

Baboons live in large, mixed-sex troops of about 50 members. The troop is led
by the dominant male, who gets to eat first and has the choice of mates. He
establishes his position first by fighting his rivals, lashing out with canine
teeth, and then through shows of aggression. Bonds between group members
and a hierarchy (pecking order) in which older animals dominate younger ones
is maintained by grooming, as shown here.

▲ CHANGING LEADERS

Most deer that inhabit open country live in herds, which are single-sex for
much of the year. The tight-knit group of females is mostly led by a dominant
hind (female deer), while males form looser bands. During the breeding season,
stags (male deer) clash to win control of the female herd, with which the
winner then breeds. When mating is over, the stag rejoins a band of males.

▲ DEFENSIVE CIRCLE

In the Arctic, musk oxen live in mixed herds of 15-20 animals. Group life
provides the young of these large goats with safety from predators such
as wolves. When a wolf pack approaches, the oxen form a circle with their
calves inside. The adults face outward with long, curving horns at the ready.
If an ox leaves the group to charge the attackers, the others close ranks.

COMMUNICATION

Communication with others of their kind allows mammals to find mates and rear their young. Mammals that live in groups communicate to coordinate the hunt for food, and warn of danger. Social mammals, such as wolves, chimpanzees, and dolphins, use a range of complex signals to interact with other group members. The senses of various mammals are fine-tuned to different messages, including visual signals, body language, scents, touch, and sounds.

FACIAL EXPRESSIONS

FEAR
Chimpanzees live in groups in which a strict pecking order extends from older to junior members. These mammals use a range of facial expressions to convey their place in the group. A young chimp intimidated by a senior shows its fear by opening its lips while clenching its teeth.

SUBMISSION
Junior chimpanzees calm their elders after a squabble using an expression that signals surrender or submission. The young chimp produces a pouting smile with its mouth half-open, with a face that signals "please don't hurt me." The expression resembles a human forced smile.

EXCITEMENT
When young chimps are playing, they show their excitement with an open mouth that shows the teeth, but looks relaxed. The young animal screams and grunts as well. In addition to facial expressions, chimps use more than 30 sounds to interact with others, including shrieks, roars, and hoots.

◄ DANGER SIGNALS
Visual signals and sounds can protect herds from danger. Antelope, such as these lechwe, graze on aquatic plants. If frightened, they run into deeper water with their tails raised, exposing their white rumps as a warning to others in the group. Other mammals, like white-tailed deer and rabbits have a similar method of raising the alarm when danger threatens.

BODY LANGUAGE ►
Wolves live in packs of 8-20 members with a strict chain of command between senior and junior animals. The hierarchy is reinforced partly through body language and also through sounds such as growls and whines. High-ranking wolves show their status by holding their heads and tails high, with ears pricked. Juniors express submission by cringing with ears flat and tail held between the legs. During a confrontation rivals show aggression by snarling and baring their teeth.

communicate

Hackles (neck hairs) are raised to look as frightening as possible

Junior wolf signals defiance by snarling with its ears back

High-ranking wolf asserts dominance with ears pricked and tail held high

◄ TALKING THROUGH TOUCH
Touch is a good way of communicating at close quarters. Mutual grooming occurs between friends and is a purely social activity, which zebras and horses find relaxing. It strengthens bonds between members. The advantage of standing head to tail while relaxing is that they have all around vision to look out for predators.

DOLPHIN TALK ►
Dolphins are social mammals that live and hunt in schools of about 20 animals. Group members use a range of sounds, including whistles, squeaks, groans, and clicks, to find and catch food by echolocation and to communicate with each other. Each dolphin has its own signature whistle, which it uses to identify itself and its whereabouts to other dolphins. Lacking vocal cords, it is thought that dolphins produce sound using air sacs in their nasal passages.

▲ SMELLY SIGNALS
Ring-tailed lemurs of Madagascar live in troops of 20-40 mammals. They use their striped tails to send various messages to group members, and these visual signals are often reinforced with scent. Male lemurs warn rivals away by spreading scent from skin glands over their tails and then waving their tails to waft the smell at rivals. These stink fights can last for an hour or more. Lemurs also use scent to mark the boundaries of their territories (*see page 78*), as this animal is doing.

Female vervet scolds her offspring with a snarl that shows her teeth

Young vervet expresses submission by cringing and hiding its teeth

▲ COMPLEX COMMUNICATION
Vervet monkeys are social primates of African woods and grasslands. Scientists have discovered that these mammals not only use a wide range of calls to signal feelings and intentions, but also to warn of different threats. If a vervet spots a leopard approaching through the grass, it gives a warning call that makes the others climb trees. If it spies danger in the air, such as a circling eagle, it gives a different signal that makes the troop take cover on the ground.

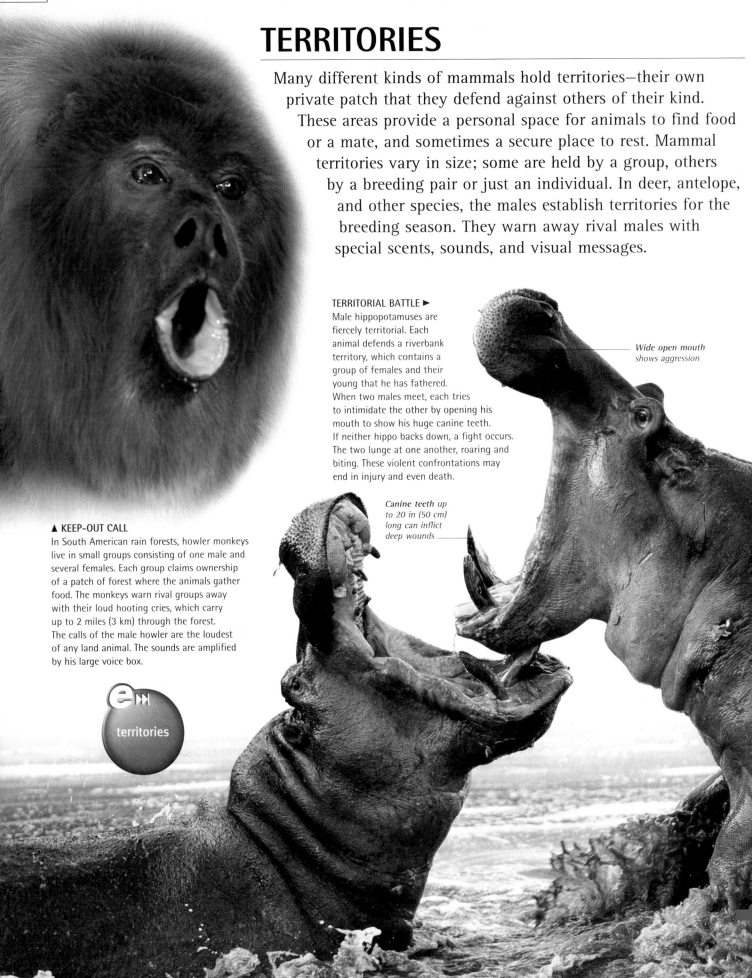

TERRITORIES

Many different kinds of mammals hold territories—their own private patch that they defend against others of their kind. These areas provide a personal space for animals to find food or a mate, and sometimes a secure place to rest. Mammal territories vary in size; some are held by a group, others by a breeding pair or just an individual. In deer, antelope, and other species, the males establish territories for the breeding season. They warn away rival males with special scents, sounds, and visual messages.

TERRITORIAL BATTLE ▶
Male hippopotamuses are fiercely territorial. Each animal defends a riverbank territory, which contains a group of females and their young that he has fathered. When two males meet, each tries to intimidate the other by opening his mouth to show his huge canine teeth. If neither hippo backs down, a fight occurs. The two lunge at one another, roaring and biting. These violent confrontations may end in injury and even death.

Wide open mouth shows aggression

Canine teeth up to 20 in (50 cm) long can inflict deep wounds

▲ KEEP-OUT CALL
In South American rain forests, howler monkeys live in small groups consisting of one male and several females. Each group claims ownership of a patch of forest where the animals gather food. The monkeys warn rival groups away with their loud hooting cries, which carry up to 2 miles (3 km) through the forest. The calls of the male howler are the loudest of any land animal. The sounds are amplified by his large voice box.

territories

▲ DISPLAY SITES
Kob antelope are among the mammals that establish territories for the breeding season. Each male lays claim to a special display site, called a lek, where he shows off to the females. Kob leks are just 50 ft (15 m) across. The males battle for the best sites, locking horns and pushing, but these contests rarely result in serious injury. Females wander through the lekking area and choose the winners as mates.

◄ SCENT MARKING
Cheetahs and many other carnivores mark the boundaries of their territories with scents, which linger for a long time after they have gone. The cheetah backs against a tree and sprays it with a smelly form of urine. Other cheetahs can tell the sex, age, and reproductive condition of the animal from its scent signal. Cheetahs also scent mark with saliva by rubbing their cheeks and chins against trees and rocks.

◄ BREEDING BEACHES
During the mating season, sea lions, fur seals, and elephant seals make their way to remote beaches to breed. The males compete for a stretch of beach where they will keep a group of females and will fight off any male that gets too close. After the territories are won, the females give birth to their pups and then mate a few days later. This male sea lion is roaring and puffing himself up in an attempt to force a female to mate.

◄ FEEDING TERRITORIES
In Indian forests, each female tiger maintains a territory large enough to hunt in. These feeding territories vary in size depending on how much food, in the form of prey animals, they contain. Each tigress vigorously defends her patch against other females, but will allow male tigers to enter. Like other members of the cat family, tigers mark the boundaries of their territory with strong-smelling urine.

HOMES

Many kinds of mammal make shelters of various kinds. Some are simple structures, others intricate balls of woven plant material, or burrowed networks that stretch far underground. Mammal homes provide protection from predators and the elements. Some species build special nursery nests where the young are born and reared. Forest and woodland mammals often nest in trees, while semiaquatic species such as otters and platypuses make their homes in riverbanks. In open country where vegetation provides little cover, mammals such as badgers and rabbits take refuge underground.

▲ LEAF TENTS OF TENT-MAKING BAT
Tent-making bats have evolved an ingenious way of hiding from enemies. They nibble through long palm or banana leaves so that they droop down or fold over to form a little tent. As many as 50 bats may shelter in each of these structures, which also shields the occupants from rain and sunshine, providing the stable conditions the bats need to rest. Some tents are shaped like tubes, cones, or vases, while others resemble umbrellas, such as the one shown here.

ORANGUTAN NEST ▶
While some mammals build lasting homes, others make less permanent structures. As orangutans move through Southeast Asian forests, they weave nests of twigs and branches to sleep in at night like the one shown here. In African forests, chimpanzees and gorillas search for food on the ground by day, but climb into trees and fashion nests at dusk to escape from ground-based predators. Chimps build a new nest almost every night.

Sleeping platform is made by interweaving branches

Outer layer of tough plant materials repels rain

▲ SQUIRREL DREY
Gray squirrels construct a ball-shaped nest called a drey, often wedged in the fork of a tree where high winds will not rock it. The outer layer is made of twigs and bark, while the inside may be lined with leaves, straw, and wool. The squirrel shapes the hollow center by turning around and around, as birds do when they build nests. Summer dreys are generally flimsy, while squirrels build stronger structures for winter. In spring, this structure is used as a nursery drey for the squirrel's babies.

▲ BADGER SETT

Badgers are among the mammals that shelter from enemies, and the weather, underground. The badger's home, called a sett, is an extensive burrow network that can descend to depths of 60 ft (18 m) below ground. Badgers use their powerful, clawed front feet to excavate these tunnels. Their ears and nostrils close to keep out dirt while digging. Successive generations of badgers may inhabit the same sett.

▲ POLAR BEAR DEN

In the icy Arctic, most polar bears stay active all winter. But the pregnant female bears dig a den in a snowdrift or the earth as the long polar night closes in. The litter of one to four cubs is born between November and January. Throughout the harsh winter, the mother remains inside the den suckling her cubs. When spring arrives the family leaves the den, and the hungry female goes hunting. The cubs remain with their mother for another two years.

homes

▼ RABBIT WARREN

Rabbits live in a burrow network called a warren, dug by the females. The dominant doe (female) and other high-ranking females inhabit the main warren. Junior females may build short burrows called stops, where they give birth to their young. At dusk and dawn, the rabbits leave the warren to nibble grass, but don't stray far from burrow entrances, so they can dive back down if they spot a predator.

Male rabbit may act as a sentry while the others feed

RABBIT WARREN

1. Entrance holes are wide enough for rabbits, but not for predators, such as foxes
2. Living chambers are connected by narrow passages leading downward or sideways
3. Warren tunnels head off in all directions, stretching for several hundred feet below ground
4. In loose soil, tree roots and stones shore up the walls of the tunnels and help to prevent them from collapsing
5. Nursery burrows are lined with moss, grass, and fur plucked from the mother's chest

MIGRATION

All types of animal travel on migrations—regular and often long, tiring journeys that are mostly undertaken to avoid harsh conditions such as extreme cold, heat, or lack of food or water. Some animals migrate to reach a favorable site to give birth and rear their young. Along with birds, reptiles, fish, and amphibians, many mammals migrate, including caribou in North America and vast herds of zebra and wildebeest across the plains of Africa. Bats use their flying abilities to make long migrations, while many types of whale, dolphin, and seal swim vast distances through the oceans.

LEMMING IRRUPTIONS

Most migrations happen at regular times of year, in tune with seasonal changes. But Siberian lemmings make irregular migrations called irruptions, which are triggered by overcrowding. In years when food is abundant, these rodents breed very quickly, until there are so many that food becomes scarce. Then huge numbers of young lemmings stream away from overcrowded sites in the mountains. The urge to migrate is so strong that they will swim wide rivers if they have to in order to find food.

▲ NORTH–SOUTH MIGRATIONS

Many mammals of temperate and especially polar regions regularly undertake long north-south journeys to avoid harsh seasonal conditions. They include caribou (reindeer), which move in vast herds up to half a million strong. These deer spend the long days of summer grazing the tundra pastures in the far north, then journey south in the fall, to pass winter in the sheltered forests of the North American taiga.

WANDERING WILDEBEEST ►

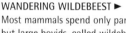

Most mammals spend only part of their time on regular migrations, but large bovids, called wildebeest, spend most of their lives on the move. These grazing beasts migrate in a huge circle across the grasslands of Africa, in search of the new grass that springs up after rain has fallen. They gather in huge herds numbering tens of thousands to journey over rugged hill terrain and cross swift-running rivers.

▲ MOUNTAIN MIGRANTS

High mountains have a harsh climate with short summers and long, freezing winters. Mountain mammals such as goats, and this chamois, make vertical migrations up and down the mountain to avoid the worst conditions. In summer they feed on grass and flowers in the alpine pastures near the summit, where there are few predators. In the fall they move down to feed on shoots, moss, and lichen in the valleys below.

OCEAN JOURNEYS ►

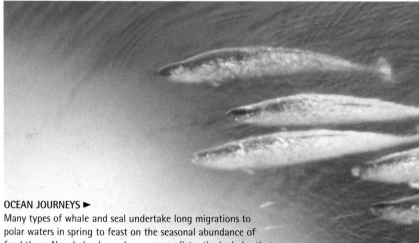

Many types of whale and seal undertake long migrations to polar waters in spring to feast on the seasonal abundance of food there. Narwhals, shown here, are small-toothed whales that spend most of their lives feeding on the edge of the Arctic pack ice. They move south to give birth to their calves in the sheltered waters of inlets in Greenland and Scandinavia. Male narwhals are known for their long, lancelike tusks.

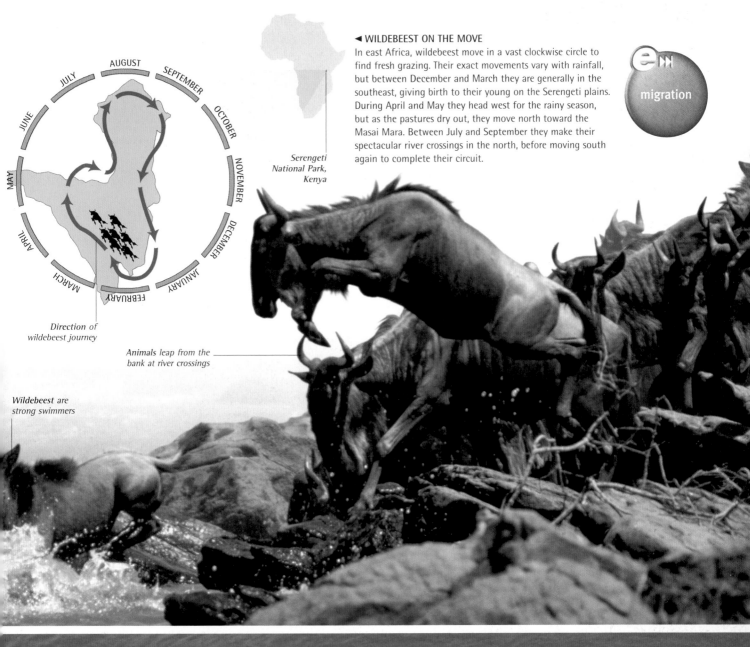

AUGUST
JULY
SEPTEMBER
JUNE
OCTOBER
MAY
NOVEMBER
APRIL
DECEMBER
MARCH
JANUARY
FEBRUARY

Serengeti National Park, Kenya

◄ WILDEBEEST ON THE MOVE

In east Africa, wildebeest move in a vast clockwise circle to find fresh grazing. Their exact movements vary with rainfall, but between December and March they are generally in the southeast, giving birth to their young on the Serengeti plains. During April and May they head west for the rainy season, but as the pastures dry out, they move north toward the Masai Mara. Between July and September they make their spectacular river crossings in the north, before moving south again to complete their circuit.

e ►► migration

Direction of wildebeest journey

Animals leap from the bank at river crossings

Wildebeest are strong swimmers

While some mammals migrate to survive harsh conditions in winter, dormice, ground squirrels, and many bats have a different tactic. They stay where they are but enter a deep sleep called hibernation. In the safety of the nest, cave, or burrow, they spend months in a state of unconsciousness from which they seldom rouse. In cold, bleak conditions, mammals have to eat a lot of food to survive and keep warm. When food is hard to find, it makes sense to conserve energy by resting in this way. Other mammals, such as bears, pass winter in a lighter state of sleep called torpor.

Hibernating dormouse feels cold to touch

Store of nuts will provide energy when dormouse wakes in spring

▲ HIBERNATING DORMOUSE

Dormice, like this one, spend up to seven months each year hibernating. Through the winter months they remain inactive and do not feed, surviving on a store of body fat. In addition to dormice, true hibernators include flying squirrels, marmots, and many bats. All are relatively small mammals, with a large surface area compared to their body mass. This means they lose heat more quickly than large mammals and therefore need more energy to keep warm.

HIBERNATION SITES ►

In temperate regions, bats pass the winter in hibernation, with their wings folded over their bodies to conserve heat and moisture. In sheltered roosts such as caves or hollow trees, these little animals cluster together for warmth. Even so, their body temperate drops to within a few degrees of their surroundings. Some species can survive subzero temperatures, while others migrate vast distances to reach a favored site to sleep.

Ground squirrel gorges on berries in the fall

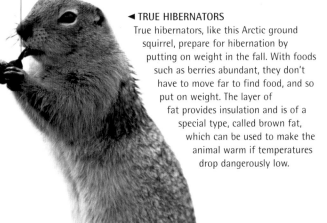

◄ TRUE HIBERNATORS

True hibernators, like this Arctic ground squirrel, prepare for hibernation by putting on weight in the fall. With foods such as berries abundant, they don't have to move far to find food, and so put on weight. The layer of fat provides insulation and is of a special type, called brown fat, which can be used to make the animal warm if temperatures drop dangerously low.

BODY FUNCTIONS OF A TRUE HIBERNATOR—DORMOUSE

	HIBERNATING	ACTIVE
HEARTBEAT	1–10 BEATS PER MINUTE	100–200 BEATS PER MINUTE
BODY TEMPERATURE	35–50°F (2–10°C)	95–104°F (35–40°C)
UNCONSCIOUS	CONTINUOUSLY	SLEEPS BY DAY
WATER LOSS	ALMOST NONE	IN FECES AND URINE
BREATHING RATE PER MINUTE	LESS THAN 1 BREATH	50–150 BREATHS

During hibernation, a dormouse's body processes slow right down to save energy. Pulse and breathing fall dramatically, as does the production of waste materials. The little animal's temperature cools almost to that of its surroundings, so it feels cold to the touch. In fact, it looks dead, yet its body is not completely inactive. Part of the brain that is still alert will trigger a survival mechanism if the dormouse is in danger of freezing, directing body fat to be burned to create heat.

A FEW MINUTES AT A TIME

16 HOURS A DAY

20 HOURS A DAY

▲ GIRAFFE SLEEP REQUIREMENTS

Like the deep sleep of hibernation, daily sleep saves energy and refreshes a tired animal's mind and body. Different mammals require varying amounts of sleep, partly depending on their diet. Plants are relatively low in nourishment, so large herbivores like giraffes have to spend most of their time eating. Giraffes snatch only a few minutes of sleep at a time.

▲ SLEEPING LIONS

The diet of predators such as lions is rich in protein. These carnivores only have to feed once or twice a week to keep going. Between feeds they spend a great deal of their time resting, stretched out on the ground in a relaxed pose. With few enemies except people, these animals can afford to sleep much more deeply than nervous prey animals, but they can still rouse quickly if disturbed.

▲ SLEEPING SLOTH

In South American rainforests, sloths hang upside down from the trees on which they feed. Unlike some herbivores, they spend little energy searching for food. However, their food is low in nourishment and hard to digest. Sloths save energy by only moving slowly and spending up to 20 hours a day asleep.

sleep

◄ LONG WINTER SLEEP

In cold northern habitats, brown bears spend the winter months snoozing in their dens. They can spend up to six months of the year asleep, yet most scientists do not consider them true hibernators. This is because their body processes do not slow down as much as in smaller species such as bats and dormice. Although its heart beat slows to 10 beats a minute, the bear's body temperature drops only slightly, and it can rouse itself quite easily. This lighter state of sleep is called torpor.

WAKING UP ►

In spring, the changes that took place in a hibernator's body in the fall are reversed. Breathing, heart rate, and other body processes speed up and the animal wakes up. In some hibernators these changes take place at very regular times of year, regardless of unseasonal weather such as warm spells. North American groundhogs, like this one, are famous for waking at almost exactly the same date in February each year.

REMAINING ACTIVE ►

In the mountains of North America, pikas live among the heaps of broken rock, called scree, that collect at the foot of steep slopes. Marmots, which inhabit very similar terrain in other mountains, spend the winter months in hibernation, but pikas remain active all year. They survive the harsh winter months by gathering piles of vegetation in summer. These stockpiles dry out to form nutritious hay in winter when other food is scarce.

HUMANS AND MAMMALS

Twenty thousand years ago, all mammals were truly wild. Humans hunted mammals, and mammals sometimes hunted humans as well. But about 10,000 years ago, things began to change. People discovered how to tame mammals such as dogs, sheep, and horses, turning them into animals that were easier to manage. By controlling mating between animals with the most useful features, people gradually created the first domesticated breeds. Today, domesticated mammals play a huge part in human life. We farm mammals for their milk, meat, and wool, and, in many parts of the world, mammals are also used for their muscle power. Mammals are used in sports, and many are kept as pets.

Owners are treated as pack leaders

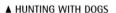

▲ HUNTING WITH DOGS

This ancient sculpture from the Middle East shows a group of Assyrian hunters setting off with a pack of dogs. At the start of the hunt, the dogs would be unleashed, so they could chase deer and other game. Dogs are descended from wolves, and they were probably the first mammals to be domesticated, about 10,000 years ago. Like wolves, dogs have an instinct for living in packs. They treat their owner as their pack leader, which makes them relatively easy to control. However, when strangers approach their territory they can react aggressively—just like wolves.

humans and mammals

▲ PULLING THE PLOW

At one time, farmers all over the world used mammals to plow their fields. This illustration from 11th-century Europe shows a wooden plow being pulled by a team of oxen. These are powerful but slow mammals, and not as useful as horses, which can work for longer periods without rest. In southern Asia, water buffalo were the main draft animals. Today, tractors have mostly replaced mammal power.

▲ DESERT CARAVAN

Strung out in a line, Bactrian camels make their way along the Silk Road—an ancient trade route across Asia. Camels can be used for carrying people and goods, as well as for their meat, milk, and wool. Although they are not as fast as horses, they can travel without water and food for several days. There are two kinds of camel: the Bactrian from Central Asia, which has two humps, and the dromedary from Africa and the Middle East, which has just one hump. The Bactrian is the only one that still exists in the wild.

◀ MAMMALS IN SPORTS
Urged on by their jockeys, racehorses gallop toward the finish line on a course in Texas. People have raced horses for centuries, and today the sport is big business, attracting spectators all over the world. Racehorses are bred specially to combine stamina with speed. To succeed, they also need special training and care. Racing mammals also include camels and several breeds of dogs—most notably the grayhound. Horses and elephants can also be trained to take part in team sports such as polo.

▲ A QUESTION OF BREEDING
Standing side by side, an Irish wolfhound and wire-haired dachshund look as if they belong to different species. But like all dogs, they are descended from the same ancestor—the gray wolf. Over many centuries, people have selected dogs for different characteristics, creating more than 400 distinctive breeds. Wolfhounds were originally bred for their size and their speed. Dachshunds were bred for hunting badgers and pursuing them underground.

HEAVY HAULAGE ▶
Elephants are the largest domesticated mammals, and also the most intelligent. In southern Asia, they have been used for centuries to carry people and heavy loads. Asian elephants are used by foresters, and some are kept for ceremonial purposes and dressed in elaborate robes. African elephants can also be tamed. During Roman times, they were used in warfare, striking fear into soldiers who faced them on foot. However, unlike their Asian cousins, there are no working African elephants today.

MAMMALS IN SCIENCE

In 1996, scientists announced the birth of Dolly the sheep. Instead of developing from a fertilized egg in the normal way, Dolly was cloned from a single adult cell. Cloning creates exact copies of living things, so it could revolutionize farming, and perhaps human life as well. Mammals are also used for other scientific purposes, particularly testing new medicines. Some people oppose this kind of research, because it can cause animals harm. However, it has saved millions of lives.

CONSERVATION

In today's busy world, many wild mammals face great challenges in the struggle for survival. Some are victims of illegal hunting, while many are affected by deforestation and other kinds of habitat change. More than one-fifth of the world's mammals are already endangered, and, in years to come, global warming and a rising human population mean that more will join the list. Throughout the world, conservation organizations are working to protect endangered mammals. Some species have been rescued from the very brink of extinction.

▲ ANIMAL ORPHANS
In Southeast Asia, orangutans face a double threat. Their forest home is being cut down, and they are also caught for sale as pets. At this orangutan orphanage, on the island of Borneo, rescued orangutans are rehabilitated so that they can be released back into the wild. It is a tricky task, because orangutans have to be taught how to fend for themselves, instead of depending on humans for their food.

ECOTOURISM ▶
Off the coast of New England, tourists watch one of nature's most awe-inspiring sights—an adult humpback whale. Until the early 1980s, whales were hunted in all the world's oceans, but today commercial hunting is banned. In some parts of the world, whale-watching has become a major visitor attraction, generating money that helps to protect the whales themselves. In the future, nature-based travel, called ecotourism, could also help other endangered mammals.

Tourists can now enjoy seeing whales in their natural habitat

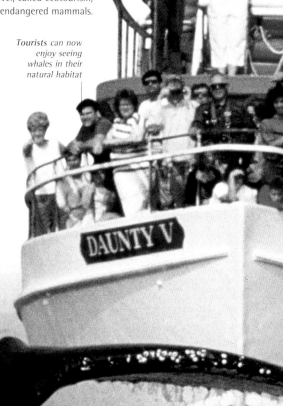

BACK TO THE WILD

PRZEWALSKI HORSE
Until the 1960s, a dwindling band of these wild horses survived in the grasslands of Mongolia, but gradually the wild herds became extinct. By breeding these horses in captivity, there are now more than 1,000, and two breeding groups were established in Mongolia in 1992.

PERE DAVID DEER
These deer, from China, became extinct in the wild in 1939. Luckily, Père David, a French missionary, had sent some deer to Europe before this and they bred. Père David's deer were reintroduced to China in the late 1980s, and there are now plans to reestablish them in the wild.

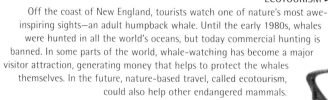

ARABIAN ORYX
With its elegant horns and tasty flesh, this desert antelope was hunted to extinction in the wild. During the 1950s, captive herds were set up in the Middle East, in the US, and in Europe. Today, there are more than 2,000 captive animals and more than 500 living wild in Oman and Jordan.

DAUNTY V

Elephant tusks were collected and burned to prevent their illegal sale

conservation

▲ ANTI-POACHING MEASURES

In July, 1989, Kenya's Director of Wildlife, Richard Leakey, organized a giant bonfire of elephant tusks. The tusks had been seized from poachers, and the ivory would have been worth at least $3 million if it had been illegally sold. The blaze made headlines around the world and drew attention to the harm caused to Africa's elephants by the ivory trade. Today, the ivory trade is banned but, despite armed patrols in wildlife parks, poaching still goes on.

ENDANGERED SPECIES

GOLDEN LION TAMARIN
With its flame-colored fur, this squirrel-sized monkey is one of South America's most endangered primates. Its home is the Atlantic forest of Brazil—a habitat that has shrunk by more than 90 percent as trees make way for farms and cities. Today, there are about 1,000 animals left. Half of them are in captivity, where they are being bred for future release.

WEST INDIAN MANATEE
Looking like floating barrels with flippers, manatees live along coasts and in rivers and feed on underwater plants. They are sluggish animals, which puts them at risk from boats. Many adult manatees have deep scars from where they have been hit by propeller blades. The West Indian manatee is classed as vulnerable, meaning that it faces a serious risk of extinction in the wild.

BACK FROM THE PAST

With modern technology and breeding techniques, it may be possible to recreate extinct mammals. Although this has not yet happened, scientists have come close with an animal called the quagga. The quagga was a subspecies of the plains zebra that lived in southern Africa. After years of being hunted, the last specimen died in 1883. Today, breeders are trying to recreate the quagga by choosing plains zebras that have quaggalike features—particularly the quagga's characteristic black and brown stripes.

In the future, DNA from long-dead animals might be used to bring mammals back from the past. However, to revive a species, scientists would also have to revive its habitat and its way of life—something that would be very difficult in the modern world.

MAMMAL CLASSIFICATION

Subclass prototheria *Egg-laying mammals*

Order	Common Name	Families	Species	Distribution	Key Features
Monotremata	Monotremes	2	5	Australia and New Guinea	The world's only egg-laying mammals. Four species, known as echidnas or spiny anteaters, live on land and have short legs, long snouts, and are covered with sharp spines. The fifth species, called the platypus, is semiaquatic. It has a streamlined body, webbed feet, and a leathery ducklike beak.

Infraclass METATHERIA *Pouched mammals*

Didelphimorphia	American opossums	1	78	North and South America	The most widespread American marsupials, found as far north as Canada. American opossums live mainly in forests and woodland. One species—the yapok—is the only pouched mammal that lives in water.
Paucituberculata	Shrew opossums	1	6	South America	Shrewlike marsupials found in grassland and scrub in the Andes mountains. Like true shrews, they feed on insects and other small animals, and have poor eyesight but sensitive whiskers and a keen sense of smell.
Microbiotheria	Monito del monte	1	1	Chile	A mouselike pouched mammal with a short muzzle, large eyes, and a thick prehensile tail. It is the only surviving member of an order that is otherwise extinct.
Dasyuromorphia	Quolls and relatives	2	71	Australia and New Guinea	A varied group of carnivorous marsupials, including quolls, antechinuses, numbats, and the Tasmanian devil. They live in a variety of habitats and hunt at night.
Notoryctemorphia	Marsupial moles	1	2	Australia	Burrowing pouched mammals that bear a striking resemblance to true moles. They live in sandy ground and feed on insects and small reptiles.
Peramelemorphia	Bandicoots	2	22	Australia and New Guinea	Ratlike marsupials with slender bodies, pointed muzzles, and long tails. Bandicoots live in a range of habitats—from deserts to forest—and eat animal and plant food.
Diprotodontia	Kangaroos and relatives	8	136	Australia and New Guinea and neighboring islands	The largest and most diverse group of marsupials, containing kangaroos, wallabies, koalas, and wombats, as well as gliders, cuscuses, and brushtails. Most feed on plants and carry their young in well-developed pouches.

Infraclass EUTHERIA *Placental mammals*

Carnivora	Carnivores	11	283	Worldwide except Antarctica. Introduced into Australia	Mammals with teeth that have evolved for grasping prey and cutting meat. Most are predatory, but the order also includes species such as bears and raccoons, which have omnivorous or plant-eating lifestyles.
Pinnipedia	Seals, sea lions, and walruses	3	34	Worldwide	Streamlined mammals with flippers that are close relatives of land-based carnivores. Seals and sea lions feed in water, but come onto land to rest and to breed.
Cetacea	Whales, dolphins, and porpoises	11	83	Worldwide	Legless mammals that are completely adapted to life in water. Unlike seals, whales and dolphins have nostrils on the tops of their heads and a single pair of limbs. Toothed whales hunt animals individually, but baleen whales filter their food from the water.
Sirenia	Dugong and manatees	2	4	Tropical coasts and rivers	Barrel-shaped mammals that spend all their lives in water and feed on underwater plants. They have a large muzzle, a single pair of flippers, and a horizontal tail.
Primates	Primates	10	372	Worldwide in tropical and subtropics, except Australia	Long-limbed mammals with forward-facing eyes and fingers or toes that originally evolved for climbing trees. They include omnivores and plant-eaters, as well as some species that live mainly on insects.
Scandentia	Tree shrews	1	19	Southern and Southeast Asia	Small squirrel-like mammals with pointed snouts and bushy tails. Tree shrews are equally at home in trees and on the ground and feed mainly on insects, catching and holding their prey with their hands.

Order	Common Name	Families	Species	Distribution	Key Features
Dermoptera	Colugos	1	2	Southeast Asia	Plant-eating mammals that glide between trees, using wings made of flaps of elastic skin. Colugos can glide for more than 155 ft (50 m). When they land on a tree, their gliding membranes fold in along their sides.
Proboscidea	Elephants	1	3	Africa and southern Asia	The world's largest land mammals, with pillarlike legs, large ears, and a long prehensile trunk. Elephants are plant-eaters, using their trunks and sometimes their tusks to collect their food. The African savanna and forest elephants have recently been recognized as separate species.
Hyracoidea	Hyraxes	1	6	Africa and the Middle East	Compact rodentlike mammals with stubby toes and small ears. Hyraxes are good climbers, and they live either in forests or in rocky places. Highly social, they spend their lives in family groups.
Tubulidentata	Aardvark	1	1	Africa—south of the Sahara Desert	A large grassland mammal with a piglike body, long ears, and long square-tipped snout. The aardvark is nocturnal. It feeds on ants and termites, breaking open their nests with its powerful claws.
Perissodactyla	Odd-toed hoofed mammals	3	20	Africa, Asia, tropical Americas	Grazing or browsing mammals that typically have one or three toes on each foot. The order includes horses, zebras, and asses, as well as tapirs and rhinos.
Artiodactyla	Even-toed hoofed mammals	10	228	Worldwide except Antarctica. Introduced in Australia	Grazing or browsing mammals that typically have two or four toes on each foot. This order includes wild pigs, hippos, camels, and deer, and also bovids—a family that contains cattle, antelopes, goats, and sheep. Many of these animals live in herds and rely on keen senses and speed to avoid attack. Several have horns or antlers.
Rodentia	Rodents	24	2,105	Worldwide except Antarctica. Introduced in Australia	The largest order of mammals, including squirrels, mice, rats, porcupines, and many other species. Rodents are generally small and have sharp incisor teeth that can gnaw through food and other materials.
Lagomorpha	Hares, rabbits, and pikas	2	83	Worldwide except Antarctica. Introduced in Australia	Rodentlike plant-eaters, often with large ears and good, all-around vision to help them see any predators. Hares and rabbits typically live in open places, including tundra, grassland, and deserts.
Macroscelidea	Elephant shrew	1	15	Africa	Shrewlike animals with long legs, a bounding gait, and a pointed snout that looks like a miniature trunk. Elephant shrews live in open places and woodlands.
Insectivora	Insectivores	6	451	Worldwide except Australia and Antarctica	Small mammals with narrow snouts that feed on insects, earthworms, and other small animals. They include hedgehogs, shrews, moles, and solenodons.
Chiroptera	Bats	18	1,033	Worldwide except Antarctica	Flying mammals with leathery wings made of skin. The largest bats—flying foxes—have good eyesight and feed mainly on fruit. The remainder feed mainly on insects, finding them by echolocation. Bats are often sociable, roosting and breeding in caves and hollow trees.
Xenarthra	Anteaters, sloths, and armadillos	5	31	North and South America, Africa, southern Asia	Mammals with specialized backbones—an adaptation originally evolved for digging. Modern xenarthrans include armadillos, whose bodies are covered in bony plates, and leaf-eating sloths, which spend their lives in trees.
Pholidota	Pangolins	1	7	Africa—south of the Sahara Desert, southern Asia	Scale-covered mammals with prehensile tails, long snouts, and sticky tongues. Pangolins feed mainly on ants and termites, using their strong claws to break open their nests.

GLOSSARY

Abdomen In mammals, the part of the body containing all the organs except the heart and lungs.

Adaptation A feature that helps an animal to survive in its environment.

Antler A bony growth on the head of a deer.

Aquatic Describes animals that live in water.

Arboreal Describes animals that live in trees.

Baleen The fringed, horny plates that hang inside the mouths of whales, such as blue and humpback whales, which are used to strain the mammal's food from the water.

Binocular vision A type of vision in which both eyes face forward, giving an overlapping field of view. This allows mammals such as primates to judge depths and distances well.

Bipedal Mammals that walk on two legs.

Blowhole The nostrils of a whale open into a blowhole at the top of the head. Some species have a single nostril, others a pair.

Blubber A layer of fat found under the skin of many mammals living in cold climates, and which provides insulation. Aquatic mammals such as whales and seals have a thick layer of blubber, as do polar bears.

Brachiation A mode of locomotion used by tree-dwelling primates that involves using the arms to swing from branch to branch.

Browser A herbivore that feeds on shoots and leaves of trees and shrubs, as opposed to grass.

Camouflage The colors and patterns on the skin of mammals and other animals that provide disguise, helping them to blend in with their surroundings and so conceal themselves from predators or prey.

Canine A sharp-pointed tooth at the front of the jaws of many mammals that is used for piercing and gripping. Also refers to dog family.

Carnassial tooth Opposing cheek teeth in the upper and lower jaws of carnivores that act like scissors, cutting through flesh and bone.

Carnivore A mammal of the order of Carnivora. Also any animal that mainly eats meat.

Carrion The remains of dead animals that form part of the diet of some mammal scavengers.

Cartilage A tough, rubbery tissue found in mammals' joints, the windpipe, nose, and growing bones.

Cell One of the tiny units of which living things are made. Some simple organisms are made up of just one cell; mammals' bodies are made up of billions of cells.

Cellulose A tough substance that forms the cell walls of plants. Mammals cannot digest it.

Cetaceans The order of mammals made up of baleen and toothed whales, and that includes porpoises and dolphins.

Class In scientific classification, a major group of animals that contains one or several orders.

Classification A method of identifying and grouping living things.

Cloven-hoofed The divided hoof of a pig, goat, cow, or deer, which consists of the two middle digits of the foot.

Colony A group of animals of the same species that live together and may share tasks such as finding food and rearing young.

Deciduous Trees that shed their leaves in the fall to conserve energy and sprout new foliage in spring. Also, the first set of teeth of mammals, followed by the permanent dentition.

Digitigrade A mode of locomotion that involves walking on the toes, without the heel touching the ground.

Diurnal Describes an animal that is active during the daytime and sleeps at night.

Dormancy A period of inactivity.

Drey A squirrel's nest, built in a tree.

Echolocation A technique that allows mammals such as bats and dolphins to find their way and locate prey. The mammal emits a stream of high-pitched sounds and then listens for the echoes that bounce back.

Endoskeleton The internal skeleton of vertebrates such as mammals, made mostly of bone in mammals, but also of cartilage.

Endothermic Animals that can control their body temperature and maintain it at a higher level than that of their surroundings. Mammals and birds are endothermic, or warm-blooded.

Epidermis The outer layer of a mammal's skin.

Eutheria The large subclass of placental mammals, to which most mammals belong.

Evolution The process by which all living things gradually adapt (change) in order to become better suited to their environment. Evolution takes place over many generations, not within the lifetime of individual animals.

Estivation A state of deep sleep that allows some mammals to survive drought or hot weather. Echidnas and susliks are among the types of mammals that estivate.

Extinction When all the individuals in a species die out so that none survive.

Family In scientific classification, a family is a group of species that are closely related.

Femur The thighbone of a mammal.

Fetus An unborn baby mammal developing in the uterus or womb.

Flipper A paddlelike limb used for propulsion.

Fossil Evidence of past life that is more than 10,000 years old. Fossils include animal and plant remains, footprints, and even droppings.

Gestation The period between mating and birth during which young mammals develop in the mother's womb, or uterus.

Gland An organ of the body that produces substances, such as hormones, that have a specific purpose.

Grazer A herbivore that feeds on grass.

Guard hair One of the long, coarse hairs in the fur of many mammals that repel the elements.

Habitat A particular type of environment in which mammals and other animals live. Deserts and woodlands are examples of habitats.

Harem A social group made up of a male and at least two female mammals. Some mammals form harems just for the breeding season.

Herbivore An animal that eats plant food.

Hibernation A state of deep sleep that allows mammals such as dormice to survive cold weather. During true hibernation a mammal's body temperature, heart rate, and breathing slow considerably, and it is very difficult to rouse.

Hormone A chemical that circulates in a mammal's blood to regulate certain body processes. Hormones are produced by glands.

Incisor Teeth at the front of the mouth used for biting, gnawing, and grooming.

Incubation In monotremes and birds, the period during which the mother warms the eggs with her body heat.

Infrasound Sounds that are too low in pitch for human ears to hear.

Insectivore A mammal of the order of Insectivora. Also any animal that eats insects.

Irruption An irregular journey undertaken by mammals such as lemmings in response to harsh conditions or overcrowding.

Keratin A tough protein found in mammal hair, nails, and horns.

Kidneys Body organs that filter waste products from the blood.

Kingdom In taxonomy, the first and largest grouping into which living things are divided. All life on Earth is grouped into five kingdoms: animals, plants, fungi, protists, and monerans.

Lagomorphs The group of mammals that contains rabbits, hares, and pikas.

Lek A shared display area used by male mammals such as antelope during the breeding season, in an effort to outperform their rivals and win mates.

Litter A group of young that are all born to a female mammal at one time.

Mammary glands The milk-producing organs of female mammals that are used to nourish the young, located on the chest or abdomen.

Marine Describes animals that live in the sea.

Marsupial A common name for one of the group of mammals Metatheria. Pouched mammals give birth to their young after a brief gestation period. The offspring then develop, usually attached to a teat in the mother's pouch.

Migration A regular, seasonal journey undertaken by mammals such as caribou, wildebeest, and many whales, among others. Mammals and other animals migrate to avoid harsh conditions, to find food, or to reach a favorable site to breed and raise their young.

Monotreme One of the small group of mammals called Prototheria that lays eggs. The group consists of echidnas and the platypus.

Natural selection A process by which evolution takes place. Animals that are best adapted to their environment are more likely to survive and produce offspring. Over time, favorable characteristics will therefore become more common.

Nectar A sugary liquid produced by flowers, which provides food for some mammals.

Nerve Bundles of nerve fibers that carry messages to and from the brain. They are important for coordinating movement and collecting information via the sense organs.

Nocturnal Mammals and other animals that rest during the daytime and are active at night.

Omnivore An animal that eats a variety of foods, including both plants and animals.

Opportunist An animal that is able to vary its feeding habits to consume a variety of foods depending what is available.

Order In scientific classification, a large group of animals that contains one or several families and forms part of a class.

Organ A major body part with a distinct role to perform, such as the heart, liver, or brain.

Organism All living things, such as a plant or an animal.

Ovary Part of the reproductive system of female mammals that produces the eggs.

Parasite An animal that lives on or inside another animal, called the host. The parasite benefits from this, but the host does not.

Pelvis A group of fused bones attached to the backbone that joins with the femur of the hind legs.

Phylum In scientific classification, a major group of animals that is part of a kingdom and contains one or several classes.

Pinnipeds The order of mammals made up of true and eared seals and the walrus.

Placenta The temporary organ that develops in the womb of many pregnant female mammals to nourish the unborn young.

Plankton The microscopic plants and animals that float near the surface of oceans and lakes and provide food for many animals, including some marine mammals.

Predator An animal that hunts other animals, its prey, for food.

Prehensile Describes the tails of animals such as monkeys, and the trunks of elephants that grip and grasp branches, acting as an extra limb.

Prey An animal that is hunted for food by another animal.

Primate A member of the order of mammals that includes apes, monkeys, and humans.

Promiscuous Describes mammals that mate with many partners during a breeding season.

Quadrupedal Animals that walk on four legs.

Regurgitate To bring up half-digested food to speed up the digestive process, or produce undigested food to feed the young.

Respiratory system The body system that allows animals to absorb oxygen into the blood, which is needed by cells to process food in order to release energy.

Rodent A member of the largest order of mammals, which includes rats and mice.

Roost The resting site of a flying animal.

Ruminant A cloven-hoofed mammal with a multichambered stomach that contains microbes that can digest tough plant material.

Savanna A tropical grassland.

Scavenger A mammal or other animal that feeds on dead remains.

Semiaquatic Mammals and other animals that live partly in water and partly on land.

Sirenians The order of mammals made up of dugongs and manatees.

Social A mammal or other animal that lives with others of its kind in a cooperative group.

Species A group of living things that resemble one another and are able to breed together and produce fertile offspring.

Spinal cord The main nerve in the body of vertebrate animals that runs down inside the backbone to link the brain with smaller nerves throughout the body.

Story A vertical layer of growth in a forest.

Symbiosis A relationship between two different species, from which both benefit.

Taiga The wide belt of coniferous forest in the far north of the northern hemisphere.

Tapetum lucidum A reflective layer at the back of the eyes of many nocturnal mammals that helps them to see in dim light.

Territory An area that a mammal or group of mammals uses for feeding or breeding and is defended against others of the same species.

Thorax The chest region of a mammal's body, above the abdomen. The thorax is protected by the rib cage.

Tissue A group of cells in an animal's body that perform the same function.

Torpor A sleeplike state of inactivity in which the body processes of some mammals slow down to conserve energy in harsh conditions. Many bats become torpid by day.

Tundra The barren, treeless lowlands of the far north of the northern hemisphere.

Ultrasound Sounds that are too highly pitched for human ears to detect.

Umbilical cord The structure that links unborn placental mammals to the blood-rich placenta in the womb.

Understory The layer of vegetation in a forest or woodland, below the canopy and above the ground layer, or forest floor.

Uterus In female mammals, the womb in which the offspring develop in the period before birth. The young of placental mammals develop in the uterus and are well-formed when born.

Warm-blooded *See* **Endothermic**

Vertebrate An animal with an internal skeleton, including a backbone. Mammals, birds, fish, reptiles, and amphibians are all vertebrates.

INDEX

A page number in **bold** refers to the main entry for that subject.

ACKNOWLEDGMENTS

Dorling Kindersley would like to thank Andy Bridge for proofreading and Hilary Bird for the index; Margaret Parrish for Americanization; and Niki Foreman for editorial support.

Picture Credits

The publisher would like to thank the following for their kind permission to reproduce their photographs:

(Abbreviations key: t=top, b=below, r=right, l=left, c=center, a = above)

2: Auscape/John & Lorraine Carnemolla; 3: Nature Picture Library/Ron O'Connor; 4-5: OSF/photolibrary.com/Daniel Cox; 8: Ardea/Masahiro Iijima (bl); 8-9: N.H.P.A/Andy Rouse (c), Seapics.com (b); 10: Getty Images/Paul Nicklen (b); 11: Nature Picture Library/Anup Shah (bl), N.H.P.A/Martin Harvey (cl), (tr), Science Photo Library/GE Medical Systems (tl); 13: Associated Press/Carnegie Museum of Natural History/Mark A. Klingler (cl); 14: National Geographic Image Collection/Jonathan Blair (cl); 16: Nature Picture Library/Dave Watts (cr), N.H.P.A/Ken Griffiths (cb); 16-17: N.H.P.A/Nigel J. Dennis (b); 17: Ardea/Ferrero-Labat (cl), M. Watson (tr), N.H.P.A/Nigel J Dennis (cr); 18: Nature Picture Library/Bernard Castelein (bc); 19: Nature Picture Library/E.A. Kuttapan (cb); 20: Ardea/Francois Gohier (bc), OSF/photolibrary.com/Mark Hamblin (t); 21: Nature Picture Library/Gertrud & Helmut Denzau (br); 22: Ardea/Francois Gohier (tr); 23: Corbis/Joe McDonald (br); 24: Corbis/Michael & Patricia Fogden (tl), Nature Picture Library/Dave Watts (br); 25: FLPA/Frans Lanting (cr), Jurgen & Christine Sohns (bl); 24: Nature Picture Library/Anup Shah (tl), Bernard Walton (cl); 26: Ardea/M. Watson (tr), N.H.P.A/Rich Kirchner (b); 27: Ardea/Masahiro Iijima (r); N.H.P.A/Manfred Danegger (tl); 28: Ardea/Ferrero-Labat (cl), Ardea/Chris Knights (b), Natural Visions/Richard Coomber (c); 29: Auscape/John & Lorraine Carnemolla (tc), Nature Picture Library/Barrie Britton (cr), Nature Picture Library/Tony Heald (bl); 30: Alamy/Martin Ruegner (t), Getty Images/G.K & Vicky Hart (cr), (cra), (bl), Getty Images/Wayne Eastep (crb), Science Photo Library/Peter Chadwick (cl); 31: Corbis/Ralph A. Clevenger (br), Corbis/Michael & Patricia Fogden (bcl), Corbis/Lester Lefkowitz (t), Corbis/Joe McDonald (bl); 32: Ardea/Sid Roberts (bc), Ardea/M. Watson (br), Corbis/Dan Guravich (t), N.H.P.A/T. Kitchin & V. Hurst (bl); 33:

Ardea/Eric Dragesco (br); 34: Alamy/Stephen Frink Collection/Masa Ushioda (tr), FLPA/Mitsuaki Iwago/Minden Pictures (bc); 35: Alamy/Stephen Frink Collection/Masa Ushioda (tr), Bryan And Cherry Alexander Photography (bc); 36: N.H.P.A/Stephen Dalton (bl); 36-37: Corbis/Tom Brakefield; 37: Ardea/John Swedberg (tl), Corbis (bl), Nature Picture Library/Dave Watts (cr), Nature Picture Library/Doug Perrine (cra), N.H.P.A/Rich Kirchner (tr), OSF/photolibrary.com/Daniel Cox (crb); 38: Corbis/Steve Kaufman (tl), Nature Picture Library/Bruce Davidson (bl), N.H.P.A/ANT Photo Library (bc); 39: Science Photo Library/Merlin Tuttle (br); 40: Ardea/Mary Clay (bc), Nature Picture Library/T. J. Rich (tr); 41: Natural Visions/Richard Coomber (bl); 42: Ardea/Paul Germain (bl),OSF/photolibrary.com/Daniel Cox (r); 43: Nature Picture Library/Peter Blackwell (bl), Nature Picture Library/Tony Heald (tr); 44: Corbis/Carl & Ann Purcell (tr), Natural Visions/C. Andrew Henley (br); 45: Ardea/Andrey Zvoznikov (cal), (cca), Ardea/Dennis Avon (tcl), DK Images/Jerry Young (tr), Nature Picture Library/Jim Clare (cl), Nature Picture Library/Brandon Cole (b), OSF/photolibrary.com/Alan & Sandy Carey (cr); 48: DK Images/Natural History Museum (bc), FLPA/Gerry Ellis/Minden Pictures (cla), The Natural History Museum, London (br), OSF/photolibrary.com/Steve Turner (ca); 48-49: OSF/photolibrary.com/Hilary Pooley; 49: Alamy/John Morgan (br); 50: Ardea /Elizabeth Bomford (cl), FLPA/Michael & Patricia Fogden/Minden Pictures (b); 51: Ardea/Pat Morris (tl), Corbis/Tom Brakefield (r), Nature Picture Library/Pete Oxford (cla), N.H.P.A/John Hartley (bl), Still Pictures/A. & J. Visage (cl); 52: Nature Picture Library/Doug Allan (b), T. J. Rich (c), OSF/photolibrary.com/Nick Gordon (tl); 53: Corbis/Raymond Gehman (cra), FLPA/Gerard Lacz (cr), FLPA/Mitsuaki Iwago/Minden Pictures (tr), Nature Picture Library/Bruce Davidson (b); 54: Nature Picture Library/Mark Payne Gill (tl); 55: Ardea/Chris Harvey (cl), OSF/photolibrary.com/Daniel Cox (tr), Still Pictures/Martin Harvey (bc); 56: FLPA/Minden Pictures (tl), National Geographic Image Collection/Warren Marr/Panoramic Images (bl), Nature Picture Library/Thomas D. Mangelsen (c); OSF/photolibrary.com/M Leach (br); 57: Ardea/Clem Haagner (tl), Corbis/Jeffrey L.Rotman (tr), OSF/photolibrary.com/Tim Jackson (bc); 58: Ardea/Chris Harvey (cr), FLPA/Gerard Laoz (l), FLPA/Philip Perry (br); 59: Ardea/Francois Gohier (t), N.H.P.A/Kevin Schaefer (c); 60: OSF/photolibrary.com/Martyn Colbeck (bc), (bl), (br); 61: Ardea/Augusto Stanzani (bl), (br), Corbis/Rod Patterson/Gallo Images (c), DK Images/Barrie Watts (tr); 62: Auscape/Jean-Paul Ferrero (bc), Auscape/David Parer & Elizabeth Parer-Cook (bl), (br), Natural Visions/C. Andrew Henley (tr); 63: Auscape/Mike Gillam (br), OSF/photolibrary.com/Farneti Foster Carol (tr), Still Pictures/John Cancalosi (tl); 64: Auscape/David Parer & Elizabeth Parer-Cook (bc), (cr), Nature Picture Library/Dave Watts (c); 65: Ardea.com/D. Parer & E. Parer-Cook (tl), Auscape/Jean-Paul Ferrero (cr), Steven David Miller (br), Nature Picture Library/Dave Watts (tr); 66: Corbis/Marko Modic (br), Nature Picture Library/Jeff Rotman (tr); 67: Corbis/Tom Brakefield (bl); 68: Nature Picture Library/ T.J. Rich (cb), Nature Picture Library/Anup Shah (r),

N.H.P.A/Jonathan & Angela Scott (ca); 68-69: Corbis/ John Conrad (b); 69: Ardea /Jean Michel Labat (cl); 70: Ardea/Francois Gohier (cl), Nature Picture Library/Anup Shah (bl), Photovault/Wernher Krutein (tr); 71: Ardea/Ian Beames (r), Corbis/ABC Basin Ajansi (bl), Nature Picture Library/Neil Lucas (tl); 72: DK Images/University College London (bcl), Nature Picture Library/Pete Oxford (bcr); 73: Ardea/M. Watson (crb), Corbis/Gallo Images (tr), Corbis/Jeffrey L. Rotman (cra), Nature Picture Library/Anup Shah (bl), (br); 74: Corbis/Yann Arthus-Bertrand (bl); 74-5: Corbis/Clem Haagner/Gallo Images (bl); 75: Ardea/Stefan Meyers (bl), FLPA/Foto Natura Stock (cr), Nature Picture Library/Staffan Widstrand (br); 76: Corbis/John Conrad (b), Nature Picture Library/Christophe Courteau (cl), Art Wolfe/Gavriel Jecan (cr), (cra), (tr); 77: DK Images/Jerry Young (b), Nature Picture Library/Pete Oxford (tr), Nature Picture Library/Doug Perrine (ca); 78-79: Nature Picture Library/Anup Shah; 79: Corbis/John Francis (cb), Nature Picture Library/Pete Oxford (ca), Nature Picture Library/Anup Shah (bl), Nature Picture Library/Bruce Davidson (tc); 80: Ardea/Jean Paul Ferrero (bl); 81: Getty Images/National Geographic/Norbert Rosing (tr), Nature Picture Library/Andrew Cooper (tl); 82: Corbis/Kennan Ward (cl), Nature Picture Library/Ingo Arndt (bl), Solvin Zankl (tr); 82-83: Nature Picture Library/Doc White (b), Corbis/Yann Arthus-Bertrand (r); 84: Ardea/John Mason (cr), Corbis/Roy Corral (br), Corbis/George McCarthy (tl); 85: Getty Images/National Geographic/Beverly Joubert (tl), FLPA/Michael & Patricia Fogden/Minden Pictures (tr), FLPA/Frans Lanting/Minden Pictures (tc), FLPA/S & D & K Maslowski (bc), Nature Picture Library/John Cancalosi (br), N.H.P.A/John Shaw (c); 86: Corbis/Archivo Iconografico, S.A (tl), Mary Evans Picture Library (cr); 86-87: Corbis/Keren Su (b); 87: Corbis/© Lucy Nicholson/Reuters (tl), Corbis/Najlah Feanny (br), DK Images/Christopher & Sally Gable (c); 88: Ardea/Kenneth W. Fink (ccr), OSF/photolibrary.com/Konrad Wothe (tl); 88-89: Ardea/Francois Gohier; 89: Corbis/Kevin Schafer (c), FLPA/Norbert Wu/Minden Pictures (cr), N.H.P.A/Martin Harvey (bc), OSF/photolibrary.com/Steve Turner (tr).

Jacket images
Front: Getty Images: Stone (cfr, cl), Taxi (cr); OSF/photolibrary.com: (cfl).
Spine: Getty Images: Taxi (c).
Back: Getty Images: Stone (cl); Taxi (cfr); The Image Bank (cfl, cr).

All other images © Dorling Kindersley.
For further information see:
www.dkimages.com